THE CHILD'S ATTITUDE TO DEATH

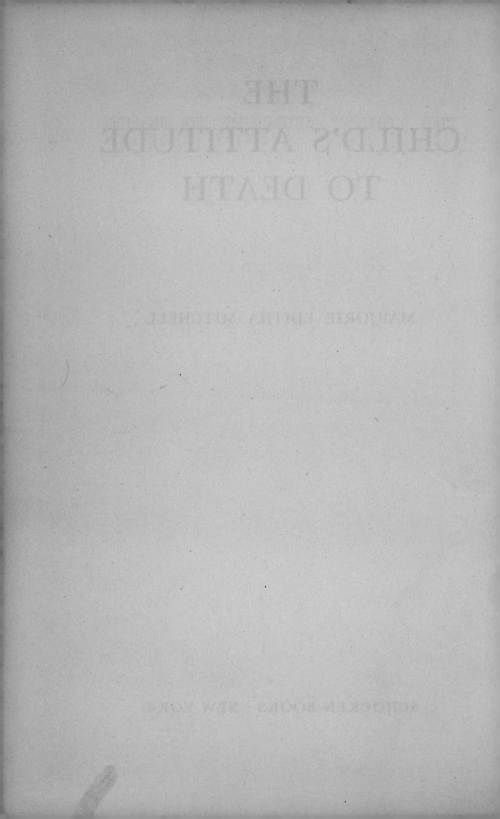

THE
CHILD'S ATTITUDE
TO DEATH

MARJORIE EDITHA MITCHELL

SCHOCKEN BOOKS · NEW YORK 1967

Published in U.S.A. in 1967
by Schocken Books Inc.
67 Park Avenue, New York, N.Y. 10016

Library of Congress Catalog Card No. 67–13156

Printed in Great Britain

CONTENTS

vi   CONTENTS

One

THE NATURE OF THE PROBLEM

Among the guardians of youth today there is an almost excessive concern over problems of sex, but the much greater problem of anxiety about death is evaded. Children's questions are often treated with embarrassed silence, or half-responses, by parents and teachers who hold no religious beliefs. In some cases non-believers feel it necessary to allay the fears of young children by fostering a faith which they themselves discarded in adolescence. Of eighty-seven teachers in training who answered a questionnaire, seventy-six stated that they thought grown-ups evaded children's questions about death.[1] When the 'normal' child in our particular culture becomes aware of death his emotional reactions can be expressed in two simple sentences—'I don't want to die' and 'I don't want you to die'. There will be occasions when he may verbalize the exact opposite under the stress of aggressive urges, but his growing understanding

---

[1] *Questionnaire given to students, 1962*

1. Do you think about your own death? (Never, Rarely, Sometimes, Often, Incessantly.)
2. Are you afraid of the act of dying? (Yes, No.) Of death? (Yes, No.)
3. Do you believe in an after-life? (Yes, No, Don't know.)
4. If your answer to (3) is negative, do you wish that you could believe in an after-life?
5. Before the age of eleven which, if any, of the following influenced your attitudes to death? (place figures, 1, 2, 3, etc, over each in order of priority). Death of a relative, death of a friend, death of pets, religious upbringing, books, films, TV and radio, conversations, rituals such as funerals.
6. Has the threat of nuclear warfare in any way influenced your attitudes to death?
7. Do you think that grown-ups tend to evade children's questions *re* death?
8. How would you, personally, answer a direct question from a child of (a) 6–7 years, (b) 11–12 years, 'What happens when you die?'
9. What is your earliest memory concerning death?

I

of the irrevocability of death brings with it mainly negative attitudes.

The main argument of this book is that death is regarded by children as a deprivation, and as long as it seems the final, unchallenged end of individual man, and perhaps of his species, it is the major deprivation. Adolescents are already asking if, in the far distant future, scientists will discover how to reverse the so far irreversible reactions of ageing and death. This is being discussed in America today more freely than here. Societies for the possible conquest of death by scientific means, such as the Immortality Research Association in California, and the Society of Anabiosis in New York, are trying to find out how to resurrect dead bodies. A recent book (March 1965) by an American physics professor, *The Prospect of Immortality*, suggesting that a way will be found to 'cure' the dead who have been kept in deep freeze has been published in this country. Adolescents with whom I have discussed this possibility in school fall roughly into two groups. One group finds the idea stimulating and full of hope; the other, comprising those who hold religious beliefs, finds that it entirely negates Christianity. Very few parents have got round to telling worried children that one day clever people may find a way to keep us all alive, though I have come across a Humanist mother recently who said she found this very consoling to her five-year-old son. The sixth-formers who see no reason for denying the possibility of reversing the death process also realize that new problems will arise in that eventuality.

Meanwhile what is the responsible adult in our society to do with regard to what appears to be an innate fear or at best a strong dislike of death in children? How can the dangers of repression be avoided? How can parents who are agnostic deal with the child whose very being cries out for positive answers?

Even those who hold some belief in an after-life are finding that with the rise of the Welfare State, and the beginnings of an affluent society, earth has become a much more desirable place than heaven. The affluent four-year-old is likely to demand television and cars in the after-life and to pity the grandad who has 'gone to live with Jesus'. Our much healthier and earlier-maturing youngsters of today accept the physiological facts of death before they are out of the infant school in many cases, and regard the dissolution of the bodies of animals and humans with both curiosity and fear. They cannot, like their half-starved and often disease-ridden counterparts of the industrial revolution period, be expected to look forward to 'being raised incorruptible'. No resurrection body could be better than their present one which lightly and brightly clothed leaps about the school playground. In Dickens' time death-beds contained children whose short and cruel lives were compensated by visions of an affluent heaven.

Autobiographies, biographies, and fiction of the nineteenth century abound in death-bed scenes of children. In the second half of the twentieth century, at least in the advanced societies of the West, it is very rare for a sibling to be deprived of a brother or sister. One might think that the declining death rate, particularly affecting the five to fifteen age group, would make today's children less anxious about death than those of earlier generations. With the near rout of the infectious diseases and deficiency disorders, if death comes it is unlikely to be a lingering one, with sorrowful relatives round the bed. It is much more likely to be caused by accidents in the home or on the road, and is usually swift, and if not, then it is relieved by drugs.

Yet my investigations into children's attitudes to death today reveal a great deal of anxiety, and if the old patterns of dying and death have changed, new ones have taken their place. The nineteenth-century child may have been aware of death in his immediate circle, but the twentieth-century child has access to television and radio and the Press, and is extensively informed, often mal-informed, of death and disasters, violence and sensational destruction throughout the world. As the earlier-maturing child passes into adolescence we find 'the supreme fear' becomes evident— i.e. the total death of *homo sapiens* by nuclear explosions. Nothing like this ever entered the conscious mind of the Victorian child.

In attempting to deal with their children's attitudes to
death when these are overtly expressed some parents and
teachers base their methods on an underlying assumption
that maturity implies a 'coming to terms with death', as if
death, like birth and puberty, is a natural and necessary
stage of human development instead of an end. They say
only the immature and disturbed really worry about death.
It is true that excessive preoccupation with death may be
associated with disturbance at all ages, but there still remains in normal children an unresolved problem which has
been neglected and which cannot be solved by natural
maturing. At one time children were expected to accept
poverty, disease, and senility as 'the Will of God', and even
today there are still parents and teachers who regard death
as ordained by some wise deity and teach children to believe
that it is a divine mystery or the gate to a better life. Others,
unable to give religious consolation to their children,
will bring them up to regard death as functional in our
society.

If everyone lived for ever, time would lose all meaning;
there would be no need for effort; birth would become unnecessary; and how boring it would all be! But they do not
reckon with the timelessness of the child's existence, nor do
they meet the needs of the adolescent who has visions of a
new society and a new space–time system. Yet another
method has been adopted by some primitive and also advanced collectivist societies. They regard fear of death as a
disease of an individualistic society. Teach the child to regard the collective as all important and he will accept that
the individual is of no significance except in so far as he
serves the group. The collective will assume immortality.
But here again we come up against the nuclear bomb. Col-
lectives may die, too, along with the species, so there is no
real consolation here either. Also, we have no evidence that
even in Stalinist Russia or totalitarian Germany the individual really accepted that the collective was all in all.
What are we left with, then? The old consolation that 'you
will live on in your children'? But this simply will not do for
today's children. In the junior school they may have come

across problems of population and breeding. On the radio recently for all ages to hear it was stated that in future the production of children, far from being a duty to the State, might be regarded as anti-social. Artificial insemination from a few desirable donors using a few selected women may become a possibility sooner than we think. Then where is our immortality? There is a danger that with the discarding of religious dogma the doctrine 'man is the measure of all things' may lead us back to a pre-Copernican state when the earth was regarded as the centre of the universe, though only, of course, in so far that man was God's creation. Twentieth-century man has to think again and think very hard about the old philosophical questions regarding human function in a universe possibly 'teeming with life'. Children's concern with dying and death cannot be dealt with except in a much wider context than our particular twentieth-century human ruminatings on this tiny planet.

This book is an attempt to discover how far present day children's attitudes to death have been influenced by the great social, scientific, and religious changes of this century, how far the bomb has entered into their consciousness, and if there is a basic insecurity which can be traced to their early awareness of death. Under the heading of Death I have included dying and killing, as it is often impossible to disentangle these ramifications in the child mind. Although in the main the observations are confined to children of primary school age I have included some observations of very young children and of adolescents, it being necessary in any study of growing organisms to look at the earlier and later stages of maturation. It has been useful, too, to question students and other grown-ups on remembered early attitudes. Indeed, in some cases these reported memories are more accurate than direct statements from children, as children may cover up their real feelings and even their fantasies vary from day to day. There is no attempt at quantitative definition, nor, except for passing references, to make explanations in terms of a given school of psychology.

Some papers have been published in psychological journals

on death anxiety, and the major research workers on child development have included findings on children's thinking about death at various stages in the maturing process, Piaget in particular. But apart from a book published in 1940 by Sylvia Anthony, *The Child's Discovery of Death*, and more recently Gorer's *Death, Grief and Mourning in Contemporary Britain* very little work on this important problem has been published outside the learned journals. Mrs Anthony's book was the result of three years' patient research on small, controlled groups, using projective tests, and her conclusions and comments are valuable.

Since then the Second World War has ended with Hiroshima and Nagasaki, followed by a long cold war, conventional flare-ups, and growing threats of nuclear deterrents. Children have heard that six million Jewish men, women, and children were killed under the Nazi régime, and they have heard of children dying of starvation in over-populated and under-developed countries. Could this happen to them? There has been a further decline in Christian observance and the grown-ups are even more hesitant and uncertain. Teen-agers have openly expressed a philosophy of 'eat, drink, and be merry for tomorrow we die'. Yet no one has really investigated one of the possible causes for outbreaks of wild destruction and personal violence. May it not be that a great basic insecurity becomes known to the adolescent on the threshold of an adulthood which thus appears completely meaningless, which ends in the incinerator? Some of the more vocal of the Mods and Rockers have indicated their fear of adulthood and its final end. Although at the moment and probably for many years to come no honest grown-up can answer a child's direct questions about death, nevertheless I believe there are methods of dealing with this basic and natural anxiety, which is, as Charles Darwin pointed out, one of the things which distinguishes man from his animal ancestors who have little or no 'foreknowledge of death'.

I shall attempt to make some very tentative suggestions for parents, teachers, and others who hold no definite religious beliefs on how they may help to alleviate this natural suffering, though they cannot hope to get rid of it. The special problem of bereavement, which has been investigated by a number of research workers, will be dealt with separately.

That there is a maturing process involved in children's attitudes to death, and that this process can be examined, to some extent, by objective tests is well established. But the determining factors which will influence the rate, nature, and end-results of this process will differ with each child. Genetic patterns will play their part, but from the moment of birth the external environment, which is a complex of physical, mental, emotional, and social factors, will modify the child's inherited and congenital make-up. The type of house and neighbourhood, the economic level of his parents, their abilities and understanding, his position in the family, the cultural pattern of his community, are some of the many variables which will act positively or negatively on the developing human organism. Parents belonging to the sect known as the Exclusive Brethren will have decided even before birth what religious influences they intend to bring to bear on the new child, and they will be supported in this by the weight of their community, while other parents, vaguely Church of England with a tendency to agnosticism, may still remain undecided until specific problems arise such as baptism, Sunday school attendance, and church.

As soon as the child extends his circle beyond the home, into the neighbourhood group and school, he will receive other influences, some supporting, some antagonizing those he first felt as an infant. Similarly with scientific influences, the child growing up in the home of scientists or scientifically minded parents will tend to develop an attitude different from those brought up by parents who subscribe to occultism. The sociological background also begins to operate at birth, sometimes before, acting as one of the determinants of early development, behaviour, and attitudes. The town child in a crowded tenement, the middle one of a large family with a low income level or an income unwisely spent, in a home with no cultural amenities, with the wrong diet, physically and mentally, may have his attitude coloured by ignorance and prejudice, as may his contemporary in a rich country house, for very different reasons.

Play, the purposeful activity of the child before he goes to school and has some of it organized for him, will vary according to the child's background, as Opie and others have shown so well. Wordsworth's 'Six years darling of a pigmy size' played at weddings and funerals and we still find the same spontaneous games among children today, but the kind of ritual they use, and indeed their attitudes to the married and the dead, will be determined by their locality, their homes, and their playmates.

In examining that part of the child's background in Great Britain today which is likely to affect his attitude to death it has been impossible to be too specialized and detailed. The backgrounds have been painted in, as it were, on large canvases with varying degrees of light and shade, colour and dimness, emphasizing this or that group of figures in the foreground. One could, instead, have taken three or four particular children and made detailed and comprehensive portraits of them in their various backgrounds and produced by this method some clear miniatures, but I have preferred to do it the other way even if the picture may at times be blurred. I have assumed that as soon as a child reaches school age to some degree he will become the 'heir of the Ages'. Schools today set out to educate 'the whole child', although only too often he ceases to be whole at seven-plus and henceforth is educated piecemeal. To educate the whole child is a very difficult task, especially today when it has to be done in a society which is in a rapid process of change. The 'heir of the Ages' may find himself in a backwater with regard to religion, science, social codes, and even methods of learning, for the school is rarely in the vanguard of progress, tending rather to be conservative, safe, even timid. His religious and scientific background may be fifty years behind the times, which is one of the reasons why adolescents may become startled when they first begin to find out for themselves what has been going on in the world outside school.

In the following four chapters I have attempted to outline some of the religious, scientific, and sociological influences which surround the child in Britain today, particularly in school, and to show how ritual, myth, and superstition still play a large part in determining attitudes.

Two

THE RELIGIOUS BACKGROUND

Between the ages of five and fifteen-plus at the time of writing 94 per cent of children in this country are educated in State schools. The only statutory compulsory subject is religious education, and the various local authorities have 'agreed syllabuses' all of which interpret religion as Christianity. Some of these have not been revised since they were drawn up following the 1944 Education Act in spite of the changes in religious thinking which have been spreading among the teachers themselves. The children also must attend a daily act of corporate worship. There are special denominational schools for children whose parents want a particular form of indoctrination, but there are no free schools for those who wish their children to be brought up as atheists, agnostics, or Humanists. Such parents must either opt out of the State system altogether and send their children to one of the few and expensive progressive schools which have no religious instruction or they may make use of the 'conscience clause' and withdraw their children from the actual acts of worship and the lessons involving religious instruction.

It is interesting to note that this clause is made use of mostly by parents who do hold religious views but not necessarily Christian ones. Humanists, by and large, leave their children with the rest on the grounds that children suffer if singled out from their fellows. We find, then, that most children in British schools today are being taught a form of Christian religion that may or may not be practised by their parents and teachers and which often uses a terminology which has become obsolete and quite unlike that used in any other lesson.

While many schools are still teaching that Jesus is the Son of God who rose from the dead the theologians are discussing Dr Robinson's *Honest to God* and 'religionless Christianity'.

With the increasing output of paperbacks on modern religious trends, together with new researches on the historical background of the New Testament and the authorship of the Epistles, the Churches are being forced to examine their 'images of God'. To Humanists much of this discussion seems to be 'words, words, words' and by the time some of the more intelligent adolescents have reached the fifth form they become aware of the semantic dishonesty of retaining the term 'God' to denote a concept that has changed out of all recognition. Their act of worship in the primary school involved petitionary prayers to a father-image, their scripture lessons described Jesus of Nazareth as though nearly two thousand years ago he was the end-product of human evolution.

Samples of prayers written by top infant children in schools with a daily Assembly in the Hall which includes the Lord's Prayer, petitionary and thanksgiving prayers, echo what these children have imbibed passively. I have never come across death, bereavement, or the after-life expressed overtly in such prayers, though illness is frequently included. The following are taken from a class *Book of Prayers* made and illustrated by the children of one infant school, age six-plus.

'Dear father god, please will you help poor sick and blind, please will you help us to be good and help us to help them and help people that fall off there motor bikes and they are in hospital and god will be with them.'

'Dear God I love you I love you so much because you put things right that's why I love you love you.'

'Dear Lord Jesus in Heaven bless all the little children who are ill and have no mothers or fathers.'

'Dear Lord Jesus please bless us through the night pleases bless the people of Peru and send the people who are in hospital home again.'

Out of twenty prayers in this book illness was mentioned fifteen times. (1963, Spring Term.)

The Newsom report voices the opinions of most teachers and educationalists in calling for a revision of agreed syllabuses in religious education, and some are already being

B

overhauled, but the same report calls for moral and spiritual education to be based on Christianity, and an 'act of corporate worship' is considered to be essential for 'half our Future'. Many teachers are being asked to sacrifice their integrity for the supposed needs of the young for a religious faith. For them, too, there is a conscience clause, but only those with very strong anti-religious views usually make use of it. Most are advised 'not to stick their necks out' while still in training college.

What actually is this religion which is influencing our children's ideas of death? We have seen that in school it is still traditional Christianity. At home it may be the faith of the parents, with or without the Church, or the faith of the Church, with or without the parents. Some parents who are non-believers send their children to church and Sunday school. The estimated number of Sunday school attendances was two million in 1964 as against five million three decades ago, and the teaching may be done by people with no qualifications whatsoever. 'Religion' is a difficult word to define. As distinct from Humanism, it implies some sort of belief in a supernatural, and it is probably true to say that all religions involve attempts at union with something other than man, whether this 'other' be in the form of gods, spirits, one Almighty, or the 'divine ground' of the mystics. To a very great extent religious experience, like artistic experience, is subjective and therefore difficult to test or prove; it is synthetic rather than analytic, individual rather than collective, although societies do arouse it collectively in mass worship, public rituals, etc. Ethical systems have been linked to it, and even based on it, but religion is not ethics. There are religions without gods and without a belief in any after-life. It is therefore not in the nature of religion itself to create these dogmas. When the glory of a spring morning arouses a feeling of oneness with 'the whole of reality'—a feeling not unknown to quite small children—the experience of wonder and awe may be described as religious. Later on I shall suggest that the fostering of such experience may be one of the ways in which we may help to allay fears of death. But too often the teaching of religious dogmas atrophies such feelings. When we begin to attach a qualifying word to religion, such as 'Christian' or 'Muslim', we have already foreshadowed the decay of that particular faith, for we have made it exclusive and limited. The religious background of our children today is already confused, unstable, in the process of being dissolved by the tide of scientific discovery. Yet if we go into our primary schools and listen to children's conversations and read their writings, watch puppet and live drama, examine their art, and carry out appropriate tests, we shall discover that their anxiety about death is evident, while at the same time they are verbalizing a belief in the Christian religion which affirms immortality.

The Christian backgrounds support a particular type of monotheism, stemming from the Hebrew faith of the Old Testament, which has always been closely linked to rigid ethical and moral codes of the 'Shall not' type. Although Jesus substituted the positive 'thou shalt love' for the negative, earlier commandments, Christianity has never thrown off its preoccupation with 'sin', which is becoming an almost meaningless term to those who are growing up in the post-Freud age. Indeed, some moralists have blamed juvenile delinquency on the loss of the sense of sin and the absence of fear of hell. Except for the Roman Catholics and some of the rarer non-conformist sects, few of our children today are taught that wrongdoing may result in eternal punishment. Yet they still sing hymns and say prayers which include concepts of religion which are not only obsolete but which no child could possibly understand. The BBC broadcasts of religious services for primary schools (spring, 1963) use such phrases as 'Jacob was the type of "fallen man" whom Jesus came to save' and 'these interludes . . . will portray him (Jesus) as setting out from heaven'. One of the hymns has the refrain:

> Alleluya to Jesus who died on the tree,
> And hath raised up a ladder of mercy for me.

The deity is referred to as the Lord or God or the Dear Father.

The custom in many infant schools today to encourage the children to write their own prayers has already been referred to. There are many junior schools which carry on with this tradition in the lower classes. The pattern is much the same. One child aged seven-plus included, 'Thank you, dear Father God, for the atom bomb which ended the war.'

There is supposed to be no compulsory religious education in nursery schools, but individual heads and teachers may introduce it either in the form of stories and songs or in simple ritual acts of worship and one may find it in local agreed syllabuses. Christmas is considered to be the most suitable season for introducing Christianity to the very young and the preparations for the Nativity may begin in October. Father Christmas is naturally discarded very early, but the religious myths with which the child confuses his fairy tales are supposed to be accepted as truth throughout his school years.

During the cold spell of 1963 John, aged three and a half, was fascinated by the falling snow and watched it with great concentration through the nursery school windows. He murmured from time to time, 'There's lots more up there.' When I asked him what else was up there he replied rapidly, 'Jack Frost, Father Christmas, God, Jesus, and that's about the lot.' Another example of confusion which may not appear at the time to be anything but a charming conversation to grown-up listeners reveals the kind of religious explanation given to a small child by adults. Two children were playing in the sand-pit in a nursery school in 1962:

JOHN (3): 'Do you know what? My Grandad's gone to live with Jesus.'

GILLIAN (3.9): 'With Jesus?'

JOHN: 'Yes. He couldn't stand the pain any more so Jesus took him.'

GILLIAN (*went on digging silently*).

JOHN: 'We'll soon go to live with Jesus, won't we?'

GILLIAN (*no reply*).

JOHN: 'We'll all go to Jesus.'

GILLIAN: 'I've never seen Jesus.'

JOHN (*looking bewildered*): 'Grandad's gone to be a fairy.'

GILLIAN (*digging silently again*).

JOHN: 'We'll be fairies, won't we?'
GILLIAN (*departs*).

(Children verbalize belief in heaven and God, but any watchful teacher soon realizes how confused these ideas are.) Tricia, George, Robert, and John were playing in the Wendy House. Linda, aged four, came to join them. Without any preamble, she told them: 'Daddy has put Rex to sleep. He's my old dog. He's in heaven. He sleeps all the time in heaven. He'll never be let out of heaven because he's naughty. Tiger, he's alive but he's asleep in heaven.' The rest looked bored and said nothing.

Two boys, aged four, were playing on the fire-engine they had made out of boxes:

JOHN: 'The fire will burn us all up.'
STEVE: 'I'll pour water on us.'
JOHN: 'Then we'll drown.'
JOHN: 'Let's shoot the fire.'
STEVE: 'Let's shoot the policeman. No, let's throw a bomb at the police.'
(*A lot of pretence of shooting and throwing bombs. A girl comes to see what is going on.*)
GILLIAN; 'Shut up you boys.'
STEVE (*yelling*): 'We've killed a policeman.'
GILLIAN: 'He's gone to God.'
BOYS (*yelling even more*): 'We've sent him to God.'

At this point the class teacher came up and diverted them to the sand-tray.

It is likely that there was less confusion in the mind of Charles Kingsley when he wrote at the age of four years, eight months the remarkable verse:

> Life is, and soon will pass;
> We . . . we rise again . . .
> In Heaven we must abide.
> Time passes quickly,
> He flies on wings as light as silk.
> We must die
> It is not false that we must rise again
> Death has its fatal sting,
> It brings us to the grave
> Time and Death is and must be.

This verse, certainly written by a precocious boy destined to become an author, and obviously repeating phrases of grown-ups, must have meant something to him. His first 'sermon', preached at the age of four, was not unusual in his day nor in the memory of the over-fifties today. 'We must follow God and not follow the devil, for if we follow the devil we shall go into the everlasting fire, and if we follow God we shall go to heaven.' Whether he had actually any concept of death we cannot say. (Tests on under-fives reveal that to them if death has any meaning at all it is regarded as reversible.) A fully developed concept of death rarely comes until adolescence, but Kingsley's mental age was probably high. Grown-ups today, remembering a similar sort of upbringing, declare that by the age of five they did have an idea of death as a door to heaven and they certainly believed in a new body with wings, for the idea of a resurrection body was constantly being dinned into them. (There is increasing evidence that children's concepts are influenced by sociological and cultural factors, including religious upbringing.) A child, also aged four, was told his grandfather had gone to live with Jesus, and queried the wisdom of Jesus in taking someone with such an old body. He was then told that when we die we have wonderful new bodies, and his immediate reaction was, 'I wonder what my new body will look like?'

The myth of the scapegoat God is so close to ancient mythologies of other cultures and has been so closely analysed by psychologists that most young teachers recognize it for what it is. Nevertheless, many of them still teach it. The Middlesex County agreed syllabus of religious instruction, still in operation in 1965, has this: 'From the first the child will be introduced to the idea that God is behind the physical universe, is responsible for it, and cares for it.' It goes on to specify the teaching which should take place in the infant and junior school. 'The Easter term carries the narrative on through the childhood and life of Jesus to his death and resurrection.' The term 'historical' is twice used to include not only Christ's death but also his rising from the dead.

The following, given to me by the mother of an advanced

four-year-old child of highly intellectual Humanist parents, reveals the concern of a happy, normal boy about death and the beginning of his attempts to deal with the problem:

'He thinks a good bit about death and it comes into his play stories. To start with he just accepted that people died the way clothes wear out or toys break, but didn't really think what that meant. Then a friend told him that God makes you alive again when you die, but since then he's worked out his own theory, eliminating God, and when he was talking about it the other day I took notes. He said: "You know, Anna, when you die, after two or three days something happens which you can't understand—a bubble comes and touches your foot and suddenly you are alive again." (*Are you the same age?*) "No, you start since you were a baby again." (*Are you the same person?*) "You're the same person, only different things happen to you." (*Are you the same family?*) "You come to a different mother and father— only don't worry because they look a bit the same, and their names are the same. Your life is a bit changed, but all the same you can do rather the same things." (*Can you remember how you were?*) "No, but you eat many things, you eat the things you should when you start growing up again." Then he told us that all this was just a story his panda had told him.'

Perhaps one of the reasons why Christianity has become the religion of death—so much so that some tribes have resisted all missionary attempts at conversion—is because of confusion between the mythological and historical, a confusion which only now is beginning to worry the makers of syllabuses. Whether Jesus existed as the man described in the Gospels or not, the 'Jesus of history' is too much a man for healthy minded youngsters to glory in his Cross. Capital punishment foreordained by God is entirely unacceptable to the thinking adolescent. 'The Risen Lord', on the other hand, is a God, and had he remained a completely mythological figure his death would have fallen into its right place in the cycle of birth, death, renewal, winter, and spring, disintegration and synthesis which is basic to life on this planet. Then the rituals which, as J. B. S. Haldane once said, are so valuable in human societies would have been able to remain in poetry, art, dance, and festivals.

A student's report on an aspect of religious education with a class of eight to nine-year-old 'B'-stream children illustrates children's confused ideas, though she, herself a Christian, did not realize what was happening. 'Having been told the Easter story, they were told to draw a picture illustrating any part of it from Palm Sunday to the Resurrection. About a third of the class drew either the entry into Jerusalem or the soldiers guarding the tomb. All the rest drew a crucifix, and drew it with extreme care and sensitivity. Discussion on the appearance of Jesus after the Crucifixion gave rise to a conversation on ghosts, etc, but the children did not seem to regard the appearances of Jesus (i.e. suddenly being in the midst of a gathering despite locked doors, sudden vanishings, etc) as being "ghostly". They seemed to regard them more as miraculous (and true) although they had called to mind ghosts.'

In answering a questionnaire in 1963, which included 'How would you answer a direct question from a child (a) aged 6–7 years, (b) 11–12 years, "What happens when you die?"' a small selected group of 105 third-year training college students returned answers. About half (56) gave religious answers. They are now teaching. To the sevens they would say such things as 'You go to live with Jesus' and to the elevens 'the earthly body decays but the spirit lives on'. Among the agnostics there is an open confession of not knowing how to answer the sevens, some adding 'it all depends on the child'; but attempts are made with the elevens —'No one really knows. Different people have different ideas. Some believe in a soul which lives on.'

A smaller batch of twenty London School of Economics students were more agnostic, only three giving religious answers. One of them elaborates for the younger child, 'The world goes on very much the same, like a pantomime which you are no longer watching,' and for the elevens, 'Stress the physical and steer clear of the metaphysical.' Some of both groups would liken death to sleep, which is very dangerous as children told this have often not dared to go to sleep.

The Study and Research Committee of Christian Education undertook an inquiry 'into the varying approaches to
religious education during the third and later years in non-
selective secondary schools', and as a result published
Teenage Religion in 1961 under the authorship of Harold
Loukes, Reader in Education in the University of Oxford.
By question and answer, discussion, and some written work
it was revealed that these boys and girls 'find their lessons on
the Bible childish and irrelevant', but are interested in religious questions. The author gives suggestions for making
the religious instruction period more 'real' for these adolescents. While objecting to a great deal of the religious
teaching which is boring adolescents, this book never for a
moment questions the truth of the Christian faith and in
one place a questioner deals with the children's concern with
reincarnation theories in the following manner:

Questioner: 'Well, this idea of being born back into the world—
would you say that it is pretty common?'
Answer: 'Yes' (majority).
Questioner: 'Well, that's an Oriental idea, not a Christian idea
at all. It comes from the Orient, from the heathen faiths, and it's
very interesting that it is so widely spread. The picture of God in
your minds is pretty blurred isn't it?'

Note the use of 'orient', 'heathen faiths', and 'pretty blurred'.
The more recent Newsom report, *Half Our Future*, Chapter
7, starts off well enough, and admits that in the secondary
school teachers may be unable to subscribe to the Christian
faith and would not therefore want to teach religion. The
report also suggests that the agreed syllabuses will have to be
revised and that there is 'much common ground which
Christian and agnostic may travel together'. But the re-
commendations at the end of the chapter are, after all, what
the committee advises for all pupils of average and below
average ability between thirteen and sixteen years of
age.

(*a*) Religious instruction has a part to play in helping boys and
girls to find a firm basis for sexual morality based on chastity
before marriage and fidelity within it. [In para 164 they concede
that there are worse sins than unchastity.]

(b) The schools have a duty to give religious instruction which is more than ethical teaching. . . .

(d) We reaffirm the value of the school act of worship as a potent force in the spiritual experience of the pupils.

So here we are back at the beginning again and a report which started off bravely ends timidly and with a decidedly insular flavour. English children, they maintain, even in adolescence, whether they are believers or not, will benefit by corporate worship.

Although individual teachers and heads may scarcely look at the revised agreed syllabuses it is rather disconcerting to find that in actual fact, while lip service has been paid to changes in religious thought by the compilers of these syllabuses, in the one quoted below not only are we back with the old terminology but even exact hours of instruction are laid down. If this was put into practice as it stands children would be educated in a religious background very little different from that of their parents or even grandparents.

Surrey County Council syllabus of religious education 1964.

Extract from the regulations:

3. In County schools the total amount of time to be devoted weekly to both religious instruction and worship shall be:

(i) For senior pupils and for juniors over the age of eight—150 minutes, of which not less than 80–90 minutes shall be used for religious instruction in accordance with the agreed syllabus.

(ii) For pupils between five and eight—110 minutes, of which not less than 70–80 minutes shall be used for religious instruction in accordance with the agreed syllabus.

(iii) For nursery classes—no fixed amount of time provided that the school day opens with collective religious worship and religious instruction is given in accordance with the agreed syllabus.

Among the aims of the syllabus we have: 'In this pamphlet it is assumed that the Christian religion is true and that all children, if they are to fulfil the purpose for which they were created, should grow up as fully practising Christians.'

Those teachers who are fully committed Christians will be able to follow the teaching syllabus honestly; others who are indifferent will probably go through the motions; some of the agnostics and atheists may decide it is better to comply and cannot do any more harm than some of the other subject syllabuses—very few teachers or children in primary schools opt out. So this is what they are committed to:

Extract from 'The Teaching Syllabus':

A. The Nursery Class Age two or three to five:

(i) The first teaching about God should be of the Heavenly Father, and his love and Jesus as our childhood pattern and children's friend. These two pictures combine to give a true picture of the one God.

(ii) There must necessarily be some teaching through practical observance, such as the prayer to be said at bed-time and at rising, and grace before meals. There also are smaller observances which may be helpful, e.g. to place the hands together and close the eyes in prayer. . . . A more detailed syllabus follows.

For infants between five and seven the miracles are included as well as death, resurrection, ascension, and the coming of the Holy Spirit. Teachers are advised to play down the horrors of the Crucifixion and are told that the hymn *There is a Green Hill Far Away* contains simple but sound teaching about the meaning of our Lord's death. This is particularly off beam considering that many children of this age have no real understanding of death anyhow.

The juniors of seven to eleven have a very long and detailed syllabus, again including the miracles and parables, and they, too, are led to recognize Jesus as minister, king, and teacher. The idea of kingship in itself may be a little difficult to grasp even though we still have a monarchy. As we are mainly concerned with young children in this book, the rest of the syllabus need not concern us except to point out that the assertion that Christ rose from the dead is put forward as a fact. 'The proof of the resurrection is found on every page of the New Testament for apart from the resurrection there would have been no writings, no gospel, no church.' Proof here is used as if it were referring to the truth of a natural phenomenon.

The Cornwall agreed syllabus (1964) states that 'for the purposes of this syllabus Religious Education is a term which takes for granted the Christian religion, not because we find none of God's truth in other creeds but because we believe that we find *all* God's revealed truth in Jesus Christ'.

It is often said that the home is more important than the school in 'laying' the foundations of religious faith, and obviously this is so where the parents hold very strong beliefs and practise the rituals of a given denomination regularly. But very few children in this country today learn religion 'at their mother's knee'. Probably the best way to sum up many parental attitudes to children and religion in 1966 is one of relief that the schools are doing the job, as it is better to be on the safe side in case God does exist and somehow children may be helped to 'behave better' if they get a spot of Christianity.

Three

THE SCIENTIFIC BACKGROUND

It is probably the introduction of more active methods of education into the primary school, followed by the trend for scientific education to start in the infant school, that will, in the end, be a major force in changing attitudes to death. Already there is considerable evidence that quite young children accept the disintegration of the bodies of animals and plants with scientific interest and associate dying with the cessation of physiological processes such as breathing, heart beats, and the inability to respond to stimuli. Though they may repeat certain religious formulæ about heaven, which they use rather imitatively, there is much less speculation about its location, fewer details about the after-life, and the 'resurrection body' appears to be a fading concept. Children who are used to finding out for themselves are more apt to question grown-ups' statements.

'How do you know?' is a question every teacher must expect today in an activity school. At one time this would have been regarded as impertinent and even punishable. Scepticism and disbelief are likely to come earlier now than in mid-adolescence. Teachers and parents will be confronted with the problem of the twelve- and thirteen-year-old brought up on scientific activity who is inclined to be nihilistic unless education includes creative activities and also fosters positive human relationships. Death, like sex, cannot be understood in purely physiological terms. The child who thinks of death as immobility is aware of one scientific aspect of human death, but if he describes it only in this way he is at an immature stage of development. Scientific observation alone will not carry him to the mature stage when he will have come to realize that 'any man's death diminishes me'.

Again, to react to stories of heaven with scepticism will

characterize the older child who has been brought up in a scientific environment, but to react without emotion and concern to the death of friends or to cease to ponder over the meaning of human life will suggest emotional immaturity.

Matthew Arnold, in the *Grande Chartreuse*, lamented:

> For rigorous teachers seized my youth
> And pruned its faith, and quenched its fire;
> Showed me the cold, pale Star of Truth,
> There bade me gaze and there aspire.

Already, it may be that students reported by their professors as anti-science have already been forced to gaze on that star too long in their childhood. Indeed, recently the dearth of science candidates for the universities has been related to the barrenness of the subject. Fear of the applications of science is often shown in adolescents. Asked if they wished they could believe in an after-life, 45 per cent of sixth-formers in a London grammar school, who said they did not believe, answered in the affirmative. ⟨Religious belief may give way to scientific discovery, but there is a danger of reaction.⟩ Children, adolescents, and grown-ups alike may accept facts yet wish them otherwise. It is no use extending science in the school curriculum if we do not realize fully all the implications. Human beings more often react against science by superstition than by religion. There is no guarantee that the child who describes death as the end, and uses physiological terms to describe the act of dying, will not grow up to personify death as the avenger and subscribe to superstitions. But as long as the majority of children in this country receive their formal education in day schools, and the home and neighbourhood are potent forces in informal education, we are probably less likely to produce generations of people indoctrinated in science in a limited sense than if the State decided that all children should be confined in boarding-schools with specified curricula.

What, in fact, is happening outside the schools? Sometimes one gets the feeling of being up to one's neck in a veritable sea of science. It is all around us and our children. If some schools are still in a backwater, the rest of society is heading for the open sea, 'and leagues and leagues beyond

that line there lies more sea'. Mothers and fathers are ab-
sorbing more and more science and technology daily, in the
home, the workshop, factory, office and profession, and in
their leisure hours. Gadgets for the home, packaged food
with precise instructions and labelled contents, ante- and
post-natal clinics, women's hour on television, the glossy
magazines, and the local libraries, all help to instruct the
modern housewife in techniques, and her baby starts life, not
as he did in the past when 'mother knew best' merely by
intuition, but mother knowing best because she has received,
and goes on receiving, help from experts. Father and son can
now buy toys which though they may appear to be only
mechanical and automatic yet test their ingenuity when they
go wrong and offer endless possibilities for improvement.

Even if the child has spent the school afternoon with
twenty others in a laboratory carrying out the same stereotyped experiment to prove Boyle's law, in the evening he may
watch a programme of photographs taken by the latest
rocket crash-landing on the moon. In the children's
libraries, which are well patronized, scientific knowledge has
been made readily available in the form of attractive books
and encyclopædias. Many of these are also in school and
classroom libraries, and children are able to buy some of the
cheaper ones, which give excellent advice on how to discover
and investigate for oneself.

Thus, outside the school the child finds himself in a
scientific background and if it is not quite so complete as that
of a child in the Soviet Union (where in the eight-year
school 35·1 per cent of the curriculum is given over to the
sciences) it is at least much more extensive than it used to be.

The English child, however, is probably well behind his
Soviet contemporary in one thing—his conception of the
Space Age. This, I think, is due to two major factors. First,
the spate of horror comics a few years ago, and even non-
horror comics of today, together with space fiction, have
distorted children's attitudes. Secondly, it was the Russians
who sent the first man into space and felt terrific pride in the
achievement. In the huge Moscow Exhibition of Economic
Achievements in the USSR (1964) one saw thousands of

young pioneers gazing in fascination at the exhibits and film shows in the section on Space Travel, and children bristled with badges of rockets and cosmonauts.

There is still confusion in children's minds in this country between faith and fact, science and religion, but judging from the older children's reactions the confusion is recognized and may be protected against. But younger children appear to be passing more quickly out of the animistic phase than did their predecessors, though it must be remembered that one and the same child may describe a classroom rabbit accurately and then listen enthralled to the story of the White Rabbit in *Alice* taking out a turnip watch from his waistcoat pocket. The magnet does not remain an object of magical properties for very long, but although children recognize that it acts in the same way under the same conditions they may also endow it with power and even the capacity for choice. Children up to nine may tell you that electricity is alive, but on further questioning it will appear to be a semantic confusion. 'You talk about a live wire,' they will say.

They do not confuse the living and the non-living as they used to do because of their greater opportunities to observe plants growing and animals moving. Children as young as five have been aware of the aliveness of plants. Sentence completion tests on eight hundred children between five and twelve designed to discover how early they associated living and dead animals with physiological characteristics revealed that by the chronological age of eight most of them associated living with breathing and moving and death with the absence of these functions. About half of the six-year-olds had also regarded death as the cessation of vital functions. This does not necessarily mean that the child has a total and adult concept of death, but it does indicate that his awareness of what happens to the body is correct.

A child brought up in a scientific environment at home, school, and in the wider neighbourhood is more likely not only to question religious beliefs but to react against authoritarianism. It is no use introducing science into the primary school and then blaming the adolescent who questions the values of our society and becomes agnostic. As educationalists we have not yet come to terms with the problems actually created by a scientific education in a society that in so many other respects is stagnant and even retrograde. (Children in our primary schools are making observations of the 'cycle of Nature', including death and disintegration, and at the same time are being taught that Jesus 'ascended into heaven'.) They watch the behaviour of gorillas in the zoo and sketch the museum dinosaurs, listen to how things began, in the same term as they pray and sing to God, the creator of man in his own image. The strange thing is that while children may learn about extinct animals and plants and the probable sequence of life on this planet the evolutionary approach has really barely started in the primary school. Instead of permeating the whole educational system from nursery to school-leaving, and into higher education too, evolution is an isolated topic in the majority of our primary and secondary schools, even in the sixth forms.

Sixth-formers in grammar and some independent schools are among the more fortunate of our adolescents for their education continues until eighteen or nineteen with the prospects of further education for an increasing proportion of them. They are becoming aware of new developments in the field of biology. The relationship of hormone, enzyme, and neurological mechanisms to emotional and mental processes has opened up the old philosophical questions concerning the nature of man. Is he a biochemical homeostatic system? If so, 'then it follows that a failure of self-regulation means death, and it is curious that death is so much easier than life to characterize—and define. In death the mechanisms of resistance have been over-stressed and can respond no longer. Apparently, therefore, death and even senescence are not necessities or inevitable consequences, and thus, attributes of life.'

Arguing the age-old problems, these older adolescents show considerable concern about advances in biology which appear 'to reduce man to a system of balanced reversible physico-chemical reactions' and death to irreversibility.

c

They are particularly worried by evidence of hormones modifying human personality and their hopes, fears, and aspirations being regarded as due to the interaction of genes, soma, and environment. Electronic brains suggest to many of them that *thinking itself* is a mechanical process, a function of the physical brain, and when the brain dies all cognition ceases. They report that while they could discuss philosophical theories relating to mind and matter with equanimity man's interference with thought and emotion by introducing drugs and injections frightens them. Are they afraid that advances in biological research will *prove* what was once to them an unpleasant hypothesis?

The cracking of the genetic code, with its far-reaching possibilities for altering the hereditary make-up of the new-born child, is also viewed with uneasiness, and the suggestion that one day death itself may be reversed is no less frightening. It seems that the last thing man wants to do is to take the place of the gods, to assume responsibility for life and death. Sixth-formers and students tend to agree that developments in physics do not worry them nearly as much as those in biology. The exploration of space, the possible discoveries of other solar systems with planets supporting life, relativity, nuclear fission, investigations of the time–space continuum, even nuclear warfare, shake them far less than the 'tinkering with man's personality' and the horrors of biological warfare.

Perhaps it is true to say that the triumphs of the physical sciences boost man's morale. There is something god-like in exploring space and discovering the mystery of the atom. The biological sciences, too, may glorify man in that they may lead him to become a creator of life and destroyer of death, but, on the other hand, they will lead him to recognize the limitations of his human brain, just as the physical sciences may lead him on to discovering greater intelligences than his own on far-distant solar systems. 'The scientific view of the universe no longer affords any room for human omnipotence; men have acknowledged their smallness and submitted resignedly to death and to the other necessities of Nature. None the less some of the primitive

beliefs in omnipotence still survive in men's faith in the
power of the human mind, taking account, as it does, of the
laws of reality.' In writing this in 1913, in *Totem and Taboo*,
Freud had not visualized the rapid growth of the biological
sciences and the possibility of man's conquering death as we
know it.

In *The Nature of Life* C. H. Waddington says:

We can scarcely claim to have anything like a satisfying scientific understanding of any natural process until we feel that we
are in a position to control it, or at least to see how it might be
controlled, even if we are not actually able to carry out the
necessary measures.

Death is just such a natural process, common to all organisms.

The older generation are apt to shudder at this scientific
possibility and to dismiss it as belonging only to the un-
disciplined imagination. In fact, they tend to evade it in
much the same manner as they evade the problem of death
itself, and may be positively discouraging if a sixth form or a
youth club discussion turns that way. Yet youth is aware of
the possibility of conquering death and will become even
more familiar with this prospect as new literature on the
subject emerges. One cannot educate children from the
nursery age onwards to take their place in a scientific society
without producing a generation of investigators who will hold
nothing as for ever beyond the reach of human exploration.
The rapidly growing science of genetics involves the physical
and biological sciences alike and most sixth-formers and
science students will have become familiar with some of the
possible applications such as the following quoted from
Darlington's *The Facts of Life*:

Suppose before I disintegrate you I take a careful record (sup-
posing this to be possible) of how all the atoms of your body are
fitted together. In short, I prepare a blueprint of the organization which is 'you'. Let us suppose further that this blueprint
survives for many centuries and eventually, say a thousand years
hence, comes into the hands of a man who is clever enough to
put atoms of matter (of which there is always plenty on hand)
back into their original arrangement. What would happen?
'You' would come alive again, exactly and precisely as you are at
the present moment. This may not be as comforting as those who

follow contemporary religions would like, but it may come as a surprise to many that there is no logical finality about death. It is true at present that blueprints of this sort cannot be made nor could a blueprint, even if we had one, be used for constructional purposes. But these are failures of techniques not of principle. It may come as a surprise even to Christians that resurrection can be placed on a logical footing. Whether it can ever be put on a practical footing is another issue, one to which we know no answer.

In our first chapter a recent book, this time by a physicist, was mentioned in connection with the possibility of reviving 'dead' bodies kept in deep freeze.

Glimmerings of what the future may hold, given the survival of the human species, penetrate now to the younger children even if the schools do not care to stray beyond yesterday. Television programmes such as the New Year *Challenge*, summing up the scientific achievements of the previous year and suggesting possible future developments, were certainly viewed by many juniors.

Unless, then, there is a regression in educational policy and practice and some sort of social disaster in this country, which will lay society wide open to superstition, we would expect the scientific background to play an increasingly important part in helping children to form their concepts of death. Provided they received a liberal education, we would expect their attitudes to dying and death to be formed without dogmas, yet to be both subjective and objective and to be recognizable in each of these aspects.

We might also expect adolescents to include value concepts in their interpretations of the meaning of life and death on this planet.

Possibly the more daring among these future adventurers might begin to 'crack the code' of death and discover whether it is necessarily irreversible.

Four

CHANGES IN THE SOCIOLOGICAL BACKGROUND

The impact of the sociological background on children's development is receiving a great deal of attention today, and recent surveys by such workers as Douglas, Brian Jackson, and Dennis Marsden have provided evidence that educationalists in the past may have seriously underestimated it. (Social factors play an important role in determining the rate of physical, mental, emotional, and social growth as well as in personality formation.) A child's total sociological background, including the inter-relationships between family, neighbourhood and the wider culture, may be more important in determining attitudes and beliefs than his inherited and congenital capacities, though these, varying from individual to individual, may account for some of the differences we find when examining children from very similar environments.

Compared with a century ago the most important major change which has affected children's attitudes to death in Britain is the rise of the Welfare State. In spite of, perhaps even because [of, two world wars in the twentieth century, life has become infinitely more desirable than death. If we read some of the nineteenth-century religious tracts for children, we find that misery of life on earth is contrasted with happiness in heaven.

A Sunday school tract, *A Child's Guide to Holiness* (1819), says:

Fear not, thou dying child, though life's day is drawing to a close, though the clock is quickly ticking out the few hours that remain to you of earth. Life on earth is misery compared to the joy that shall be yours in heaven.

Even in the poorest sociological area today it would be

rare to find a child able to believe this, though an adolescent may still be driven to despair by adverse social conditions. These may no longer include absolute poverty. On the contrary, there may be a high income level in otherwise poor environmental conditions.

Social class which still exists in British society is less likely to determine a child's attitude to death than it did at the beginning of the century, though expressions of fear and anxiety, together with a greater preoccupation with death by violence, as shown in some of the investigations I have made in schools, do appear to vary from class to class. But there is nothing like the miserable anticipation of a wretched end which must have haunted the deprived children of the early part of this century. I have never come across a child dreading a pauper's grave and though some of the poorer ones may show a great deal of concern about the mother having a raw deal in life there is no actual terror of death by starvation. Yet less than a hundred years ago this was so. In *The Listener*, December 28, 1961, the first of Peter Laslett's three talks on English society in 1901 starts with a significant quotation:

> Rattle his bones, over the stones,
> He's only a pauper whom nobody owns.

The article continues: 'Sixty years ago, when Victoria died at the outset of the twentieth century, one person in every five could expect to come to this, a solitary burial from the workhouse, the poor law hospital, the lunatic asylum.' In fact, even the children of the better-off classes were threatened with ending their days in the workhouse if they refused to develop the Puritanical virtues of thrift, hard work, punctuality, chastity, and sobriety. Death was not just death to these children, it might be disgraceful death. To the poorer children who were in and out of the workhouse anyhow there was no added disgrace in dying in it. Nearly 40 per cent of the children in this country were destitute in 1901. Rowntree's famous social survey of York in 1899, together with Charles Booth's on London, found that 'destitution was the outstanding characteristic of industrial society'. Already, when the Act of 1870 which made elementary education compulsory was implemented, it was found that 10 per cent of the children could not profit from schooling owing to malnutrition, and a much larger proportion were suffering from the listlessness which springs from poor physical condition. In some parts of rural England the position was far worse. Peter Laslett quotes: 'In 1903 two-fifths of the inhabitants of Ridgemount, a village in Bedfordshire, were living in poverty.'

Indeed, it was only with the planning of the Welfare State during the Second World War and its implementation after it that most children could hope to grow well nourished and able to take advantage of opportunities. As late as 1936, when Rowntree investigated York again, 31 per cent were still living in poverty, this time due mainly to unemployment, but in 1951, with the flourishing of the Welfare State, when Rowntree made his third survey of York, only 3 per cent were destitute, and these were mainly the aged.

Up to the First World War, and in many schools even much later than this, as Ethel Mannin points out in her *Confessions and Impressions*, in the elementary schools the poor children sat apart and were known, to their faces, as 'the dirty children'. I remember using the expression myself as objectively as if I were discussing the colour of a rabbit. This was the time when children sang:

> The rich man in his castle,
> The poor man at his gate,
> God made them high or lowly
> And ordered their estate.

God also decided whether you were to die of scarlet fever at the age of six or live to be ninety.

The better-off eased their consciences by telling the poor that in the final count God was no respecter of persons; king and pauper alike came to dust and faced the judgment, and if you belonged to the 'deserving poor' you might have even a better chance of going to

> Jerusalem, the golden
> With milk and honey blest

than if you had spent your days on earth in riotous living.

Infantile mortality was 94 per 1,000 in the middle class in 1899. In the poorer groups it was 247 per 1,000. Peter Laslett says: 'One baby in every six died in the working class generally. The small coffin on one of the family beds, or on the table, or under the table when the family had a meal, this was a sight every working man must have seen, every working woman have grieved for.' What, then, must every child have feared, deep down, perhaps suppressed, repressed, covered up in jokes, superstitions, rituals? We must remember that this same child, eating his 'piece' (bread and grease) standing up by the table while the breadwinner probably ate what available protein there was, in the company of a coffin, had been at school all day in a class of seventy trying to digest a mixture of the three Rs, *Grimm's Fairy Tales*, heaven and hell, and knowing one's place in society. Only a few years previously he might have been even less fortunate, for it was in the second half of the nineteenth century that Elizabeth Barratt had written *The Cry of the Children*.

It must be remembered that we have very little written records of these children's attitudes to death, for most of them grew up illiterate or semi-illiterate if they grew up at all. Most of the autobiographies were written by men and women who had a more fortunate childhood. Today, when it is fashionable even for young people to produce their life-stories and when nearly all are literate, we have much more material to draw on. Dickens, the ex-blacking warehouse boy, was preoccupied with poverty and death, but he is one of the few sociological fiction recorders of his time.

Sylvia Anthony's investigations in *The Child's Discovery of Death* deal with children just before the Welfare State had become a reality. Have there been marked changes in attitudes since poverty has declined? What other changes have been most marked? The decline in the death rate has been due to two major factors: (1) the improvement in environmental conditions such as sanitation, higher standards of living; and (2) increased scientific and medical knowledge.

Referring to the Registrar General's *Statistical Review of England and Wales for 1962*, published by HMSO, we find figures for death rates per 1,000 living, in age groups, and infant mortality per 1,000 live births, 1841–1962. Infant mortality declined from 153 in 1841 to 21·4 in 1962. Deaths at age five declined from 9·05 to 0·41, at age ten from 8·29 to 0·34, at age fifteen from 7·48 to 0·65.

Analysing further into causes of death, under fifteen years from principal epidemic and general diseases, we note a striking decline between 1851 and 1962.

Scarlet fever, as a killer, declined from 2,282 per million of the population in 1841 to 7 in 1949 and 2 in 1962; measles from 1,082 to 8 in 1962; whooping cough from 1,319 to 2 in 1962. The standard mortality rate of TB dropped from 1,438 in the period 1851–60 to 28 in 1962.

The average child today is in a very different position from that of his forebears at the end of the nineteenth century or during the first part of the present century. Not only will he rarely see a sibling die, he will rarely see one born. Birth control, having spread throughout England, the average family today is 2·2 children. Again, even his grandma is unlikely to die during his childhood (her life expectation is seventy-three years at age one year), his grandpa may just make it now that his expectation of life is a little less than three-score years and ten (*State of Public Health*, Pt 2, 1963, HMSO). In two schools under investigation the children who referred to the death of grandparents were, in the main, Jewish. In one case death had been by violence in a concentration camp.

(The child, then, will be less familiar with 'death by natural causes' than his predecessors were.) But he may come across this, at one remove, as soon as he is old enough or interested enough to read newspapers and watch documentaries on television. (He may then become aware that death from famine and disease is still operating in other parts of the world. His first-hand experience of death is much more likely to be death from accidents.) If his brother dies, the most likely age will be in mid-adolescence, as soon as he can obtain a license for a motor-cycle; or alternatively, he may be an under-five, having been burnt in the home, swallowed poison, or fallen from a table. Sudden, violent death rather than the protracted death-bed, scene with weeping relatives, doctors, and fading hopes. Death presented to him on television also will be violent. It will be killing rather than dying—shooting, knifing, drowning. Likewise, he will be present at fewer rituals. He may even be unaware of any if he lives far enough away from a burial ground or crematorium. Except in a few 'pockets' in certain areas and among certain social groups, the dead now are quickly disposed of without fuss. Mourning periods, even in the Royal Family, are now curtailed, and among the higher social grades wearing black, lowering blinds, and baked meats are out except among those who belong to a special religious sect. However, there are these pockets.

In an overcrowded, derelict area between Kilburn and the Harrow Road, the headmistress of an infant school described a funeral which had taken place in 1959. The grandmother of one of the children—or maybe the great grandmother (she was not clear which)—had died and as she looked out of her office window she saw a tremendous funeral procession. She said that in this district people will spend fabulously on the dead. She calculated that there must have been about £100-worth of flowers. There was a vacant chair made entirely of sweet peas, a broken wheel made of roses, and so on. Then she noticed that the letters were facing the wrong way and appeared to be backwards. 'Love to Nana', 'For dearest Gran', etc, were upside down. Being concerned with her children, who by now were pressed to the windows or in the playground drinking in the beautiful sight, she went out and asked why the letters were the wrong way round, and was told, 'Granny Robinson is in heaven, not on the earth, so the words must face the sky.'

In country districts, too, one still comes across ritualistic burials, but the number of simple cremations is increasing everywhere. Part A of Tom Harrison's *Britain Revisited* is prefaced by a picture showing two tombstones, one old style and one new, in Worktown's largest cemetery. The old one is a large ornate cross, the other a simple scroll. On page 43 of this fascinating book by one of the original founders of Mass Observation we find a heading 'Death, the Changer', and the observations are so relevant that they are worth quoting at some length:

Before World War II re-instituted mass slaughter of humans in 1939 an elaborate set of socio-economic interests in Worktown centred on the expectation (never quite certainty) of death and with arrangements to associate the eventual departure with what then seemed proper circumstance. No other observance during an ordinary human life was so elaborate, expensive, or emotionally surcharged. The treatment of birth often bordered on the off-hand.

And speaking of the changes:

Twenty years ago a person was left at home after death. Now 90 per cent use a chapel for the period between death and disposal . . . It used to be 95 per cent burial and 5 per cent cremation . . . In 1960 cremations outnumbered burials by over 2·1 . . . Cremation, in particular, has introduced a new idea of the departed.

Surveying the religious beliefs and behaviour of Worktown (Bolton), Tom Harrison and his co-investigators found little anti-religion, but also little churchgoing.

So the children growing up in Worktown in the sixties will find the dead quickly whisked off to a chapel of rest, placed in a simple coffin, and cremated with the minimum of ritual compared with that experienced in their parents' and grandparents' time. They will not have to dwell on the appearance of the waxen corpse on the bed surrounded by flowers, nor meditate on grandma lying in the earth with the worms until she turns to bones. Grandma is in a decent urn, or scattered to the winds to be made 'one with Nature'. It is more difficult to imagine the resurrection of the body in these circumstances.

In the *Guardian*, August 20, 1961, the sermon of the Rev Harold S. Goodwin at St Giles-in-the-Fields, Holborn, was reported:

The disposal of the dead in days when people were buried in churchyards was reverent, dignified, and purposeful . . . largely to suit the convenience of undertakers it was becoming usual to bypass the church and substitute a makeshift service in a chapel at the cemetery or crematorium . . . modern practices have little reverence or dignity and are turning the disposal of our dead into an embarrassing sanitary exercise, which leaves behind it an intolerable litter of freehold dumps for meaningless monuments.

It would seem, then, that to the child and adolescent of the sixties death should appear to be more remote than to one of his forebears of a hundred years ago, or even before the Second World War. The child in the sixties may not have the same compensations as the earlier ones—the hope of a definite heaven if he is good, the consolatory rituals; but then, he may not need them to the same extent. Will not the Welfare State help him to a happy maturity? And old age —often dreaded more than death itself—will it not be farther off and, when it comes, softened by drugs? The Victorian child was made fully aware that he might never grow up. What of the modern child?

An interesting cartoon appeared the day after the USSR exploded the 50-megaton bomb. Two small boys were pictured talking together. The caption read 'What are you going to be *if* you grow up?'

An adolescent, consoling my aunt who remarked sadly, 'Old age is creeping on,' said at once: 'Age has no meaning at all today. The expectation of life is the same for all of us.' But the death which might come is entirely man-made. No longer is God held to be responsible.

The modern child in England today will not see children dying of starvation, nor will he be compelled to read Dickens at eight, as I was. But what is the difference in attitude, if any, of the eight-year-old reading the following and the eight-year-old seeing children of the Congo on television? The quotation is from *The Old Curiosity Shop*. Little Nell and her grandfather are begging for food.

'Do you see that?' returned the man hoarsely, pointing to a kind of bundle on the ground. 'That's a dead child. I and five hundred other men were thrown out of work three months ago. That is my third dead child and last. Do you think I have charity to bestow or a morsel of bread to spare?'

And the television programme on children dying of starvation in the Congo: 'This little emaciated two-year-old-boy will die without immediate supplies.' A week later. The supplies came too late. The child died.

Though the child in the Congo may be more remote than the child in Dickens it is impossible to say which might have the greater impact on the emotions. The Dickens child is fictional, though his counterparts in real life were only too numerous. But the Congo child could actually be seen by watching children, as a reality, here and now; and so could some of the victims of atrocities in Stanleyville, for example, where children were not spared. Though his first-hand experiences of death may be fewer, though the child today may never view the corpse of a relative, or be present at ritual killings and ritual burials, though his reading books at home and school will not be spattered with death-bed scenes and holy words, nevertheless he may witness death every day on the screen or read in the newspapers accounts of murders, accidents, revolution, floods, famines, and earthquakes.

In a report on *Television and the Child*, Himmelweit, Oppenheim, and Vince drew some tentative conclusions: 'The less stylized, the more personal and realistic the portrayal of violence and the more play is made of the emotions of aggressors, victims, and spectators, the more disturbing the programme. It is not the amount of injury caused which determines the emotional impact, but rather the manner of its presentation.' The same report found that insecure children are more susceptible, and girls more than boys. Older children and the more intelligent can also be very insecure.

In the nineteenth century and the earlier years of this one middle- and upper-class children, especially girls, were shielded from 'the seamy side of life', even from society itself. As late as eighteen, or even twenty-one and over, if they were unmarried girls they may have remained at home sheltered from the world. In some cases even their reading matter was vetted. They were allowed to see and to know only what grown-ups thought fit for their young eyes and ears. Today children are part of society from the moment they can read the headlines, watch television, absorb the advertisements. Some years ago a man, Caryl Chessman, was sent to the electric chair, after a twelve-year fight against his sentence. On the wall opposite one of the schools I was investigating were the words 'Oh, Caryl'.

There was a minor outcry in a local paper because

members of the National Society for the Abolition of Capital
Punishment had given a propaganda talk to prep school
boys. But boys and girls of thirteen and under can be found
now at political meetings, nuclear disarmament demonstra-
tions, collecting for famine relief; and in top junior classes
the level of debating on civic, national, and international
problems may be very high.

With the school-leaving age at fifteen-plus, and about to
rise, with the 'rat race' for places in grammar school and
university, one would expect the child today to have little
leisure in which to read widely and meditate on life and
death. But compared with children of the industrial revolution, who worked in the mills for long hours until they rolled
under the benches with exhaustion, the modern child has not
only more hours to spare but is in a fitter state to make use
of his leisure. And though we may deplore the amount of
time which children spend on passive viewing or reading
comics, and adolescents on gang fights, dancing, and making
love, nevertheless the majority of young people appear to
show a much greater awareness of social, ethical, moral, and
religious problems than previous generations, who were
either too tired and underfed to care or who had been conditioned to believe that these matters were for grown-ups only
and grown-ups always knew best. Attitudes to death among
the underfed may be apathetic and under extreme stress
conditions fatalistic. The happier and more aware children
of today who may overtly express a fear of death are not
more disturbed but probably more healthy.

A brief reference must also be made to another big change
in English society—the development of urban and suburban
areas and the spilling of the population over the countryside
near the great towns. Conurbation brought the population
of Greater London to 8,210,000, Birmingham to 1,093,000,
and Glasgow to 1,069,000 in 1960 (annual abstract of
Statistics). Four times as many people live in towns as in
rural areas, and the 1961 population of the United Kingdom
was 52,673,000 as compared with 38,237,000 in 1901 and
15,472,000 in 1821. Children growing up in these unwieldy
'forests of bricks and mortar' are surrounded by man-made

things and space is diminished. 'Nature' is a pet to be confined to parks and gardens. The great religions and mythologies without exception are founded on Nature worship in some form. The gods do not live in offices, factories, and blocks of flats, but in the sky, trees, thunderbolts, in deserts, wildernesses, and by the rivers. The towns known to Jesus, Buddha, Mohammed, and Confucius were country towns compared with our conurbations. Zeus, Odin, Jehovah, Allah—in whatever form men worshipped God he was spacious and leisurely.

It is easier to believe in God in the country than in the town; even those who have 'lost their faith' have sometimes found it restored, or at least reduced to agnosticism rather than atheism, in the presence of Nature; country children in rural schools tend to accept religious teaching more simply and for a longer period than town children. 'Fair seed time had my soul,' Wordsworth tells us in *The Prelude*. It was in the Lake district that the boy had his intimations of immortality. There is room for a great deal more research on the different attitudes of children in urban and rural schools, but it will have to be done quickly for already the village children can get easy transport to the towns and attend nearby cinemas, to say nothing of the television set at home or at the neighbour's.

Finally, a more subtle, but probably an equally important change affecting children which has been mentioned in Chapter 3, *is the diminishing role of the father in the family*. Between the World Wars social services were already helping to eliminate the worst forms of poverty, and starvation such as Dickens described was very unusual, but the menace of unemployment darkened particularly the working classes. Children in the North, ill-nourished, ill-clothed, but kept alive by father's dole and from the worst effects of sickness by national insurance schemes, felt the degradation suffered by older brothers falling in 'love on the dole' and by the chief breadwinner who no longer had the authority which sprang from 'an honest day's toil'. Working-class wives in some districts had a long tradition of doing some work outside the home, but the father was regarded as the stable, permanent, and chief earner. The death of the main breadwinner parent had always meant that the children in the family might suffer a greater sense of loss than in any other sort of bereavement. To children in the period of unemployment the loss of work was experienced in some cases as almost equivalent to death, and death with dishonour at that. There was a social stigma attached to unemployment in spite of the fact that it was not the fault of the individual. Women in the First World War had already entered into gainful employment outside the home, and this trend continued. In some cases in the twenties and thirties the male parent was on the dole, while the mother was the main breadwinner. Now, in the sixties, there are two breadwinners in many families, in all classes, and mother's work outside the home, except perhaps in the North, is regarded as important as the father's.

In a book, *Married Women Working*, by Jephcott, Seear, and Smith, which analyses employment of wives and mothers in Peek Frean's factory in Bermondsey, the authors find that the majority of the women, being part-timers, are able to enjoy both family life and the companionship at work. Only 63 out of 7,100 children 'at risk' were delinquent in one year. On the whole, the children were happy, healthy, and able to enjoy holidays, cars, and luxuries out of mother's money. Indeed, it is mother now who provides the daughter with the party dress which once she had to wheedle out of father.

Over half the married women in this country are in employment outside the home, and this is likely to increase as the single woman over twenty-five disappears from our society.

Since the ratio of the sexes is altering and males are losing their scarcity value, their status is changing. This loss of status of the male has been cited as one of the reasons for juvenile delinquency, which is largely a male problem. However that may be, it is certain that there is a decline in patriarchal religion. God, the Father, cannot mean the same to those who do not regard the earthly father as in any way superior to other members of the family. Even mothers of babies and young children are able to work.

To some extent, both parents, together with other

'authoritary' figures are losing status. It will be some time before the full impact of these sociological changes on religion and philosophy can be known, nor can it be determined as yet how far such changes may actually be responsible for producing pessimism or optimism as the prevailing mood in a new generation. Temperament, which may be related to congenital as well as environmental factors, will certainly modify a child's attitude to death, but his temperament is more likely to be 'sunny' under good social conditions. The late Teilhard de Chardin believed that faith in man's future, which is the chief characteristic of the optimist, is absolutely essential for the survival of the species. If optimism prevails, and it can do so only under favourable social conditions where life is regarded as worth living, children will naturally come to regard death as at best a quiet end to a fulfilled life. With the disappearance of the dominant father figure, God, as an all-providing and all-sustaining deity, will also disappear and we shall no longer find children believing that they or their relatives can be saved from death by supernatural powers or be 'given' a place in heaven. According to their individual temperaments, they may grow up to subscribe to one or other of the two major beliefs about man's role in the universe which may prevail in the last half of the twentieth century. One is elevating man to the position once held by God at least in some of his aspects as Creator, Preserver, and Knower. Man, discovering how the universe works, imitating, replacing, altering, sustaining, and creating, arbiter of his own destiny, capable of 'surpassing himself' and becoming superman, is one image which is taking the place of that of the Heavenly Father on whom his children depend.

The other stands man up against the wall of the cosmos and finds that he is so infinitesimal that he cannot be measured at all. His insignificance is shared by his planet, which is less than the dust among the millions and millions of galaxies in space, the duration of which is less than a fraction of a second in cosmic time.

One might expect those who are beginning to hold the first viewpoint to be positive, active, optimistic, scientists

D

rather than artists, and the others to be negative, passive, pessimistic, and their attitudes to death to vary accordingly. If social man's great aim is to conquer the universe and build for his species a happy and maybe eternal home in it, death will be a problem to be solved; but if the universe will always remain a mystery, and unconquerable, then death, too, is more likely to be accepted as inevitable.

Five

MYTH, RITUAL, AND SUPERSTITION

The decline of myth and ritual, like that of religious belief, is characteristic of older, advanced human societies, and this decline is often associated with a flare up of exaggerated cults and superstitions such as the cult of the dead which Jessica Mitford has described in *The American Way of Death*.

In this country there has been a change in death rituals during this century. There is less emphasis on farewell ceremonies, funeral rites, and memorials to the dead, though lately there has been some attempt to revive them for commercial interests. To agnostics myths about the dead will be indistinguishable from religious belief though distinct from superstitions. Yet here and there superstitions still linger and are expressed and often modified by children. But when the infant stage is passed the writings, art, and dramatic play concerning death tends to be imitative rather than fantastic and derived from comics and television rather than with death rituals as such. From time to time, however, particularly in schools where there is time for 'free activity', one comes across children forming spontaneous groups and acting out death rituals. The two quoted below were recorded on the spot.

The first example was written down by a student who was watching a group of six girls between six and seven years of age (May 1962):

SHE DIED IN SPRING

The children dressed up before they decided anything about the play, which was Lynda's idea. The title came first—the play was fitted to it. The children practised this for about an hour in the corridor and then asked if they could do it for the rest of the class.

Lynda came on first, followed by the others.

'Go to sleep, my children,' she said.

Vonny, Norma, Katrina, and Pauline all dressed up and lay down in a row. She then took Jane by the hand and pacing the stage twice took her to the children and said, 'Kill her' (name not heard, but rather strange), pointing to Vonny.

Jane stabbed her and went off.

Lynda then said, 'Wake up, my children. Come and see . . . is dead.'

They all followed her to see . . . (Vonny) lying on the ground.

'Let us carry her to the grave and worship.'

They carried Vonny across the stage, laid her on the ground, and all went down on their knees to worship.

'Now, children, go to sleep,' and they all, including Vonny, went and lay down again.

The whole thing was repeated from beginning to end, till all the children had been killed. In each case the killed one came alive again and went to worship with the others. The last time they were ordered to sleep, Jane was told to sleep also.

'Now we will kill the master who has killed all of us,' and Lynda and Vonny stabbed Jane.

'Look, my children. This is the master who killed us. We have killed him. Let us take him to the grave,' said Lynda, 'but we will *not* worship!'

We all thought that this was to be the end of the play and were about to clap, but Lynda stopped us. They then all joined hands (including Jane, the master) and danced.

The rest of the class were rather amused by the whole thing and thoroughly enjoyed it.

Lynda was the only one who spoke at all, except for Jane, who said, 'Yes,' in answer to her commands.

Lynda called her play (so she told me later) after the title of her mother's library book. She did not know anything of the story however.

Here we find no detailed rituals associated with the corpses, but there is a feeling that death must be associated with some ceremony, dancing, or worship, and there is a common element found in all ritual—repetition.

The second example contains much more ritual and it is interesting to note that it arose in connection with a real incident and that a 'real' emotion was present.

The incident took place when I was visiting a day 'progressive' school in a morning in spring in the late fifties to talk about opportunities for scientific activities for young children. In this school the first half of each morning was free for the children to choose their own activities, and there was an open access to classrooms and gardens so that children between the ages of five and eleven could mingle with other than their own age group. There was no religious observance or instruction in this school. I walked into a classroom mainly occupied by sevens to eights and was having a look at the Nature display on tables and cupboards when a bird flew in through the open door. The following is a verbatim report on what happened:

ROSA: 'Look, there's blood on the window.'

JILL: 'The poor bird's hurt himself.'

A little knot of girls gathered round the bird where it had fallen on the classroom floor. Rosa rather gingerly picked it up. By now the class teacher was standing on the fringe of the group. Jill seized her hand and said: 'Joan, can we have the little bird in the classroom and look after it? Can I get a box to make a bed?' The teacher showed Jill where she could find an appropriate box and pieces of material for bedclothes and then again retired to the fringes.

By now other children from inside and outside had joined the group, mostly the under-nines. There was some shouting and bossing until the original group with the bird had got outside and were proceeding to arrange the sick-bed. Suddenly a boy shouted, 'Oh, look!' The bird's head had dropped. For a moment there was silence, and then the same boy said, 'He's dead,' and wandered off. The first re-actions of the rest seemed to be disappointment that they could not look after the bird and have a hospital in class. It was difficult to hear this part, but after a few minutes the class teacher was again called in to the group—'Can we have a funeral?' Immediately permission was given the children cheered up and became busy. I could only record scraps of conversation.

ROSA: 'We must bury it. Go and see if the nursery will let us use their garden.'

Here the teacher intervened and said they must use their own garden. So the bird in its box was carried in slow pro-cession of about ten boys and girls to the garden and laid on the ground while John dug a grave. It was now that the rituals started.

ANGELA: 'We ought to put flowers in its coffin.'

JOHN (*looking up from the digging*): 'It's got blue in its wings. It had better have blue flowers.' Two girls went off to search for blue flowers. Meanwhile a fierce argument started between Rosa and Jill.

ROSA: 'That coffin has to have a lid. You have to nail a coffin down.'

JILL: 'No, it's awful for it to have a lid. It's awful to be shut up.'

JOHN: 'Don't be silly. It's dead, isn't it?'

ROSA (*to Jill*): 'How would you like to be buried in a coffin without a lid with all that soil all over your face.'

JILL: 'I wouldn't care a damn, you silly clot.'

PETER: 'Anyhow, I think we ought to have a cross. You should have a cross on a grave.'

ROSA: 'O.K. Good idea. Ask Paul to make one. Go on. Shout through the woodwork window. He's doing woodwork.'

Paul, shouted at through the window, agreed, but a minute later reappeared saying: 'Robert doesn't think it ought to have a cross. It might be a Jewish bird.' The rest agreed that it could be, with the exception of John, who said they were crazy, and he had finished digging. By now the girls with flowers had returned and were arranging them around the bird. They also had a lid and without further protests from Jill the coffin was placed in the earth and very rapidly, and with obvious relief, covered over by John.

An uneasy silence was followed by Rosa's saying, 'You sing something at funerals.' They decided on 'Speed bonny boat', and in the middle of the first verse the bell went for music in the hall. The children scattered to get instruments, etc, and all but one rushed across the grass to the hall. This was Chris, aged seven. He came up to me while I was lingering by the grave.

'Mrs M, what has happened to that bird? Who is that bird?'

'Well, who are you, Christopher?'

After a moment's hesitation, 'I am my name.' Then he went on: 'I wonder if there is a part of the bird that comes out invisible and flies away.'

Knowing that this particular child had atheist parents I thought it better not to comment. As he finally picked up his recorder and prepared to follow the others he said: 'Mrs M, if I came back from my recorder lesson and heard that bird chirping again I'd drop my recorder and jump for joy all over the field.'

He was the only one who had taken no part in the rituals and the only one who had verbalized his sorrow. But one can draw no conclusions from this about the value of ritual in allaying disturbance.

A group of fifty eighteen-year-old students, asked to remember any rituals associated with death in their childhood, all reported on something, mostly in connection with dead animals—either pets or, more often, dead birds found in the garden. All the remembered rituals occurred at home and no one reported on any which had happened at school. The following are typical:

'I remember the death of my budgerigar. We made a special wooden coffin, placed him tenderly on cotton wool, and had a procession down the garden with a cross. This was very different from the death of my uncle when I was ten, which occurred a little while before. The house was in mourning, drawn curtains, black dress. I was frightened of the darkness and the silence in a house that was usually very bright and alive.'

'I remember making a cross when my pet rabbit died, and the drawn blinds when my grandmother died when I was nine.'

A student who described the 'big ceremonies' they had when they found any dead animal—hedgehogs, fledglings, pets of all kinds—and recalls lighted candles, gravestones, and long chants, also made the interesting observation: 'I also spent at least two weeks trying to bring five dead (drowned) puppies back to life. I had been told that if you stroked them you could get them alive—I dressed them up and spent fourteen days in secret with them talking to them— keeping them warm.'

Even if this memory is not entirely accurate with regard to the time she kept the dead puppies it reveals a great deal about a child's reaction to death.

It is extremely important when making deductions from the language and lore of children and primitives to relate it to environment and culture. Rituals of burial, of decorating corpses and graves, providing food and tools, singing over the body, have frequently been an expression of human hope and belief involving some sort of rebirth in another sphere. Combined with this, rituals may still be functional in acting as a direct expression of grief and an attempt to assuage it by 'Playing it out'. There may be room for such rituals even among those who hold no religious beliefs, and it may be that in withholding ritual from children in our more rationalistic society today we are producing disturbances in later adolescence.

E. O. James, in *The Beginnings of Religion*, finds the cult of the dead widespread and suggests that the ideas of an afterlife spring immediately from this cult.

Thus the idea of immortality has arisen not so much from speculations about a separable soul and phantoms of the living, as from this ritual organization of which it is the corollary. . . . Consequently it is the funeral ritual that determines the condition of the dead in the hereafter.

Whatever rituals of death may have meant to primitive man, and there is considerable evidence that they were often elaborate, prolonged, and psychologically functional, observations on children's reactions to them seem to reveal that they are usually intensely disliked, or feared, or a cause of embarrassment if they are designed by adults in connection with the death of a relative or friend. Their own rituals associated with animal death and State rituals are a different matter.

Children of my generation absorbed some of the old rituals into their games and songs, and I remember how gloomy they seemed to us. 'Cock Robin is dead and gone to his grave', 'There was a little man and he had a little gun', 'Ten little nigger boys', 'Green Gravel', and even 'Poor Mary sits a-weeping' were deathly to me, though some children

liked them. Children whispered superstitions to each other
—how you would die if you looked at chickweed in flower
or brought ivy and flowering hawthorn into the house.
Blackbirds flying into the house heralded death.

We believed, too, that 'the good die young' and looked on
with great concern at the most saintly member of the class,
taking good care not to emulate him or her.

It is noticeable in nineteenth-century autobiography,
when the death rate was high and the expectation of life low,
when children in a family might expect at least one sibling
to die early, and usually more than one, descriptions jo
death abound in ritual. We find the same thing in bio-
graphical novels and poems. Children of a later age,
reading at two or three removes, wept happily over the
deaths of little Nell, Paul Dombey, and Beth, but those more
closely associated with death in their own lives, the Sassoons,
Sitwells, C. S. Lewis, Hans Anderson, Max Ernst, and many
others, reveal that the ritual surrounding death terrified
rather than consoled them. It did not cover up the 'stark
reality' of death, nor appease the ghosts. Schoolchildren
today are not particularly interested in death-bed scenes.
Instead, they prefer death by violence.

Dr Josiah Oldfield, writing as an old man, found nothing
compensatory in the funeral rites of his childhood days:

I recall my childhood days. I see once again the black horses
trotting in front of the waving hearse . . . it wasn't poor old
John's plumed carriage that was passing slowly away that filled
my soul with fear. It wasn't the real black horses that were
quickening into a steady trot whose hoofs I heard. It was a
shadow among the plumes. It was a terrible black shadow that
was brooding, formless. I saw as in a trance the women weeping.
I saw the blinds drawn down in every house lest the blight of
Satan as he passed might curse some other villager or child. I
heard the rhythmic trotting of horses on a hard road and as they
had passed by I sensed there was a great relief, everywhere,
that we were once more safe from the King of terror.

And C. S. Lewis, in *Surprised by Joy*: 'Against all the subsequent paraphernalia of coffin, flowers, hearse, and funeral
I reacted with horror.'

Emlyn Williams in his autobiography, *George*, gives a

vivid account of viewing and touching the corpse of a young
girl when he was a child of seven:

Stiff in our Sunday best, the six of us were ushered in one by
one, out of the sun, by the hollow-eyed mother. . . . There was
one floor, and I found myself straight in the bedroom. In the
sudden twilight I could see nothing at first, conscious only of the
overpowering smell of the strange flowers everywhere, smothering
pictures and ornaments. I identified them later as carnations.
The coffin lay deep on the bed, handles gleaming opulently in
the half-dark, it looked too large for a pitiful room shrunk
smaller still in grief . . . I stood on my toes, cap clutched tight,
eyes and mouth wide with curiosity, and looked for the first time
upon Death. And Death was an exquisitely pale doll who might
at any minute creak up to a sitting position, open her eyes, and
say Mamma. But it was Kate all right; she was wearing a night-
dress like Annie's, but she will never get up, never . . . 'Cusan
Kate fach,' said a well-meaning aunt. 'Would you like to kiss
her?' I shrank back: as I had never embraced anybody it seemed
effusive to kiss a dead neighbour. But I steeled myself to put my
finger-tips to the brow, just to say I had. I had never handled ice,
and the feeling was chilling beyond imagination; the warm flower
smells and the hot bee-buzzing village shrivelled into nothing, the
world was numbered for ever.

When he got out into the village again:

Cassie and Ifor and John stood apprehensive, but more alive
than I had ever imagined anybody, gleaming, glowing, alive . . .
I shall never die, I thought, as I ate my lobscouse, never.'

Lydia Jackson, in her autobiography, *A Russian Childhood*,
also gives a vivid account of a child's reaction to dead bodies
and describes the custom of viewing corpses in Russia before
the revolution:

The bier was left open and carried high on the shoulders of
four men . . . I peered at the face in the coffin, its colour strikingly
like the wax candles we bought in church to put before the icons.
I noticed the band stretched across the forehead . . . I saw the
waxen hands folded on the chest, supporting a small holy
image . . .
The Russian peasants laid out their dead in the best room for
a three-days' vigil before taking them to be buried. All the neighbours came in to say goodbye to the dead person, and anyone
passing by could do so if he wished . . . with my knees feeling
weak, I too approached and, forgetting to cross myself, stretched
out my neck to reach the waxy hands. I touched them with my
lips, aware that the unfamiliar sweetish odour was the smell of
decay, and controlling my impulse to recoil.

The rituals of corpse viewing and corpse touching were quite common in my childhood in the villages and small towns of the Midlands, and even today it is not entirely unknown to invite children into the death chamber. I remember a schoolmate of six or seven dying and all my class were invited to go into the dead child's house on the way back from school to see 'How lovely our Lily looks'. I longed to go, but refrained, thinking quite rightly that my mother would not approve of the visit. But before afternoon school a knot of six- to seven-year-olds gathered on the ashphalt playground, top and skipping rope forgotten, to tell each other that Lily looked like a big doll, all dressed up in muslin and lace, holding white lilies, and then I knew that it was all wrong to look at Lily. They called her a doll, and a doll is immobile, and immobility is the most fearful thing about death. But later, when my brother showed me a skull, I was not upset and felt that this was real, decent, and not dressed up, whereas Lily in some way was unreal and indecent.

Even now, in 1966, students of mine say that corpse viewing is customary in some villages and when they were children it was an offence to refuse to look at the dead. We still close and weight the eyes in some cases, wash the body, clean up and plug the orifices, dress in snow-white linen, strap up the fallen jaw, and postpone the appearance of death until the coffin has been nailed, buried, and covered with earth. Children know these things. Even the body destined for cremation is prepared beforehand and the child of seven who was taken for a ride into the country to avoid the ceremony asked immediately, 'When are they going to burn Grandpa?'

The art of embalming, which is an attempt to preserve the body, is perhaps one of the most extraordinary rituals to survive to the present day. In some form preservation of the body was attempted by early man, by ancient advanced cultures, notably Egypt, and even in Soviet Russia, where it was carried out in the absence of an appropriate myth, unless the 'cult of personality' can be termed a myth. The embalmed Lenin still lies-in-state in a country which denies that

there is any problem about death. A friend of mine asked at
the Institute of Pedagogy in Moscow, 'What do you say to a
child who asks what happens when you die?' She was told:
'No child in the Soviet Union would ask such a question.
That question only comes from children with religion.'

In Britain rituals are declining, and most children today
are not expected to wear deep mourning, attend funerals,
and make frequent visits to graves with floral offerings to the
dead. But although they are no longer surrounded by the
trappings of death as they used to be when friends and
relatives died, an exception is made in the case of important
figures, such as royalty or statesmen. Fifty per cent of students asked in a questionnaire about death rituals said that
they remembered vividly those in connection with the death
of George VI. Children watching the spectacle of Pope John
being carried into St Peters Square, the solemn masses for
Kennedy, and his lying-in-state, must have learned something of the death myths which still survive in the West.
More recently we have in England the amazing mourning of
Churchill. Children, of course, are not necessarily concerned
with the myths which are the actual sources of all rituals,
but some of these have been, and are still, being taught in
schools and at home and must therefore influence children's
attitudes to death.

There are few signs at the moment of new death myths
arising. The interesting thing is that there appears to be little
connection between belief and fear of death. While rituals
may act therapeutically the actual myth which lies behind
them, whether it be of resurrection or rebirth, does not seem
to console nor to reduce the fear of death in children. In the
American Journal of Orthopsychiatry, Vol 34, No 4, a study of
the reactions of fifty-eight children between two and fourteen
who had lost a sibling showed that although all these
children felt an intense fear of death there was no evidence
that religion consoled. Where children were told that 'God
had taken away' the sibling some even feared God as a
murderer.

Six

CHILDREN'S IDEAS ABOUT DEATH

The child discovers death and examines its phenomena before it understands its significance. A certain degree of maturation has to be reached before there is any realization of its finality, and the culture into which the child is born will determine to a considerable extent his beliefs about what happens after death. Also, in a society like ours where in many families parental influence is still strong, at least until adolescence, individual opinions may divert the child so that he is able to hold beliefs which may be against the main stream of those held by his neighbourhood or even his nation. This would not be likely in a closed society such as a primitive one or a totalitarian one.

Young children, before the age of four or five, recognize death as a change of state whenever it comes to their direct notice in an organism which hitherto had behaved differently. Animal death is recognized before plant death, although some children even as early as three years have commented on dead flowers. But to nearly all young children death first comes to their notice when they discover in the field, street, or garden a dead bird, insect, or mammal. The evidence of the senses reports that an organism which was capable of self-propulsion becomes immobile. In fact, immobility to the child of this age is almost synonymous with death. During the war very young children were observed screaming and shaking their dead mothers after an air raid. Other factors, other fears were at work here, but the children's terrors included that of the sudden change to immobility. What was this unknown mother who could no longer open her mouth to speak, move her arms to take the child, and get up and walk? On the other hand, Sylvia

55

Anthony reports the case of a mother falling dead with a heart attack and the child, aged two years, eleven months, calmly going to sleep beside her. But it is significant that in this case the mother died in a place associated with sleep—in the bedroom.

That immobility is usually the most significant aspect of death to the young child is shown in his play. If you are playing dead, then you lie still. If you get up, then you are alive again. Children who may have had no first-hand experience of a dead body will learn to associate immobility with death from playing shooting games with older children or from watching episodes on television. As I write a group of children ranging in age from four to eight are banging away at each other in the street below, screaming out, 'You're dead!' 'I've just killed you,' 'You can't get up, you're dead.' In children's dramatic activities from the reception class upwards, and among the older ones in the nursery school, the immobility of the dead is regarded as so significant that if a child who has been 'killed' dares to twitch a limb or move an eyelid he incurs the wrath of his fellows and on some occasions is 'killed' again, this time with a show of violence. The dead hero or villain who lies motionless and allows you to propel him across the classroom floor without stirring at all is greatly admired. He is still dead. But children of this age are so inconsistent in their attitudes that the boy who has been 'pretending dead' and then suddenly springs to life and kills his enemy is equally applauded.

A striking example of a child's associating death with immobility occurred in a Willesden nursery school the day after Churchill died in January 1965. A four-year-old boy played 'being dead like Sir Winston' for over an hour, lying prone in a box, quite still, with his eyes tightly shut. He refused to come alive even for cocoa time and was carried in still 'dead'. The teacher said he appeared to be testing out what death in a coffin was really like and immobility was the most impressive characteristic.

I saw a rather beautiful example of children expressing the silence and immobility of death in a period known as 'creative dance' in a progressive school in March 1962. They were boys and girls of seven-plus. The PE teacher told me that for some time these children had been enthralled by the Arthurian legends and had wanted to interpret them in creative dance (a kind of music and movement). Their interpretation of the deaths of the knights and ladies was non-violent—no suggestion of battle or jousting. I watched a rather beautiful movement of 'dying'—it was more like a ballet. The teacher pointed out Roland, a difficult child. He insisted on staying alive the longest and was always the last to lie down and die. At first, she said, the others protested, but later accepted that this was 'what Roland had to do'. The end of the ballet always represented death as absolute stillness. Even the children's breathing seemed minimal.

Sleep, 'the death of each day's life', bringing with it immobility, may be one of the first harbingers of death-fears in children. Tim, aged five, reluctant to go to bed, asked his baby-sitter (a student of mine) if one day he would go to sleep and never wake up again. Adults who tell children that death is simply a sleep without waking do nothing to allay children's fears; they merely cement the dreaded connection between sleep, separation, darkness, and death.

The disappearance of the body is another aspect which children of five and upwards associate with death. Under that age they are likely to believe that death is reversible and we find this notion occurring even in some six-year-olds. Disappearance may be associated with food. The child eats dead bodies or parts of them. He may be told fairy stories about a grandmother disappearing into the stomach of a wolf.

He threatens to 'eat you all up'. This is not the place to discuss various psychological theories suggesting that death at this age may be equated with 'oral aggression'. Sylvia Anthony says:

Though death is commonly equated with the end-result of aggression, not all fantasies of aggression are necessarily associated with a concept of death. Swallowing may form part of a fantasied life-cycle, of which birth, or spitting out, or vomiting up again, is the next crisis, but in which death, as a specific process, has no proper part at all, having no identity in the mind which is entertaining the fantasy. In its earliest stages the concept of death may retain much of the reversibility, or non-irrevocability; and we shall see that with some children it continues to do so.

The disappearance or disintegration of a beloved toy may be quite clearly associated with death in the mind of a child who animates it. Brothers and sisters may play on the emotions of a younger child so that the loss of such a toy may be felt as intensely as the death of a grandparent. I remember a toy lamb called 'King Kelly' which was to me beloved and alive but disintegrating beyond repair when I was four years old. My brother insisted on a death-bed scene and a funeral. Even now I shudder when I recall his words over the death-bed of this lamb. 'King Kelly dies . . . forget-me-not.' Later, when my sister, aged eight, was undergoing a serious operation and my grandmother came in, saying, 'It's just touch and go,' this phrase recalled the 'forget-me-not' one and clearly I knew then that I had discovered death at four, and it was of the same *quality* as death is to a grown-up.

Disintegration is early associated with death and will continue to be so as long as children find decaying animal bodies and as long as there are cemeteries. Village children are likely to be more aware of this, at an earlier age, than some town children, particularly if they are used to farm and field life. A village schoolmistress reported that every February they take the reception class to the churchyard to see the snowdrops, which are very profuse, many of them actually growing on the graves. Even the youngest are aware of distintegration of the dead, unlike the child quoted by Nagy who believed that dead children continue to grow in their coffins.

'There are dead people under 'ere,' a four-year-old remarked, 'lots of 'em.'

''Ow much of 'em do you think's left by now, Miss?' Most of them accepted the rotting of the buried body as obvious, though in the same class a boy approaching his fifth birthday asked 'Miss, 'ow does 'e drag 'em from 'ere to up there?' in spite of our now being in the Space Age.

Some young children are aware of the attempts to delay

distintegration by embalming. In fact, today's children, owing to new media of communication, are likely to pick up miscellaneous information on all sorts of subjects and one is never surprised by the conversations one overhears in the infant school. Their ideas of death may be confused, strange yet often very near the mark, and in 'their move towards objectivity' they may be more influenced by environmental happenings than previous investigators, such as Piaget, have found. One child brought a picture of a heart-lung machine to stick up above the Nature Table, another an account of a sex change, and one was reading out 'What is Death?' from a piece of the *Sunday Times* used to prevent the clay from messing up the table. Anyhow, the adults are pretty confused by the death of the body. When does it actually take place? Hearts stop and can be started again, vital tissues can be removed and replaced, even breathing may cease for a short time and yet the individual can be restored. It is premature to suppose that recent scientific discoveries, such as that of heart restoration and effects of freezing, can have penetrated into the general consciousness of junior and infant school-children, but in sixth form discussions references to when death actually occurs may be frequent and lively.

Up and down the country local education authorities are pushing the cause of science for the primary school. Who knows what effect this will have on children's ideas and how it may modify their thinking? While the sequences of maturation may remain, evidence is already accumulating that certain types of learning and new sources of information may speed up the actual process. Not a great deal of research has been done on the development of the child's ideas of death, but up to date there is general agreement that, as in all other aspects of the development of the child's thinking, there is a sequence of stages and that well before the age of six nearly all children are interested to find out more about death.

It is extremely difficult to discover how children's ideas of death develop when there is so much controversy over the linking of death with all kinds of fears and hopes. So much research has been directed on these aspects, especially by

E

psychologists, who are inclined to regard fear of death as psychopathic, if intense, and immature, and a sign of egocentricity if it persists into adulthood. How is one to find out, anyhow, in a culture where it 'isn't done' to discuss death in polite conversation and where children are so often carefully steered away from the problem?

Only the few have deep analysis and reveal their repressed childhood fears, and these are reported as *disturbed* people showing fear of death. All too often the conclusion is that fear of death is a sign of a disturbed personality. But the rest—those not receiving therapy—may be just as fearful. They may be ashamed to reveal their fears in answers to questionnaires. In *What I Believe* Bertrand Russell writes: 'I believe that when I die I shall rot, and nothing of my ego will survive. I am not young, and I love life. But I should scorn to shiver with terror at the thought of annihilation ... Many a man has borne himself proudly on the scaffold.' There speaks the British ex-public schoolboy. Compare this with Dylan Thomas:

> Do not go gentle into that goodnight
> Old men should burn and rave at close of day;
> Rage, rage against the dying of the light.

So conditioned are our children even today that by the time they are grown up and ready to answer questionnaires they may really believe that death has never worried them.

In *The Child's Conception of the World* Piaget states that there are four stages in the development of the child's concept of 'life'. In the first stage, ending between six and seven years old, everything functional is living. Children at six define an object by its use. In the second stage, ending about nine years, life is defined by movement, and in the third stage, up to eleven or twelve years, children distinguish between spontaneous and impelled movement. In the final stage, over twelve, children regard life as the property of animals and plants, including human beings, and distinguish clearly between animate and inanimate objects. Piaget goes on to say that in the last two stages children assign the same meaning to life as to consciousness and that the 'notion of consciousness has a wider extension than the notion of life'. This comes from an earlier work of Piaget and there is more evidence now that these age ranges are not borne out by subsequent tests on children in our schools today, though the sequences are correct. Piaget's division into sequences in the development of thinking have also come under fire. He may be putting his age for the next stage too high, even in terms of IQs. Thus the child may pass from the 'pre-operational' to the 'concrete' and 'abstract stages' more rapidly than was hitherto thought and the development of concepts may be influenced in the individual child by various environmental stimuli. Children now, quite early on, even before six, do differentiate between spontaneous and im-pelled movement, between living and non-living things, and likewise their concepts of death are more mature at this early age.

Illig and Bates-Ames, in *Child Behaviour*, referring specifi-cally to the development of concepts of death, agree with Gesel and others that by five children regard death as an end and represent it as complete immobility. Under this age it is extremely difficult to discover what meaning a child attaches to death.

Nagy found that very young children always believe it to be reversible. Gesel finds very little or no understanding of death up to the age of four, and Sylvia Anthony says that at three years no meaning is attached to the concept. Children under five will use words like 'dead', 'killing', 'shooting', 'bang-bang', 'stiff', and so forth, according to their back-ground and experience, but it is unlikely that much meaning or emotional content is there. Gesel says that the child may 'verbalize a rudimentary notion that death is connected with sorrow'. Cousinet finds that the very young child refuses to accept the ideas of death and later attempts to substitute severe but curable illness. This I have found in investigations of children's stories and puppet plays. Some of the children, asked to complete a story about a boy balancing on a fence, stopped just short of death. This was most common in the six- and seven-year-olds. The boy broke nearly everything he had, went to hospital, his mother was 'trembling with sadness', but in the end he was cured.

Round about the age of six [says Gesel] the child becomes more emotionally involved and may become fascinated by killing. This is the age for threats . . . 'I'll kill you dead. I'll chop you into pieces.' At the same time the six-year-old worries about illnesses, death of the mother, and begins to connect old age with death. He may become interested in rituals and be disturbed by pictures and stories of dying or dead animals, but he does not yet believe that he himself will die. Here again it depends very much on the child's background to what degree these preoccupations occur and what meaning he attaches to killing. Even at six a child who has seen his parents killed will have a different attitude and probably a different idea of death than one who is playing Indians and cowboys.

The seven-year-old, according to Gesel and others, has a reasonably clear idea of the causes of death and may be morbidly interested in rituals surrounding it. He may be sad and apprehensive about the death of relatives. He may deny that he himself may die, yet nevertheless he begins to suspect that he is mortal. 'Pensive seven', as Gesel calls it, was perhaps even better summed up by the author of *Alice in Wonderland* as 'a most uncomfortable sort of age to be'.

By eight years old, sometimes before, the child is interested in what may happen after death and is able to accept that death is the common lot of humanity, animals, and plants, and that one day he himself might die.

Gesel refers to the nine-year-old as one who accepts death realistically and without marked interest, realizing the biological essentials. Further investigations have shown that many children between nine and ten do show real fear of death. I, myself, remember clearly sitting up one whole night when I was nine chanting a phrase from the C of E Litany, 'Spare us good Lord,' as I thought that would save me from sudden death, which is the type of death particularly to be avoided according to the Litany. It is in the ages from nine until adolescence that children who now accept death realistically also show terror of non-existence. These terrors are usually covered up by denials, jokes, tough attitudes. The Opies give examples of children entering 'a period when death seems extraordinarily funny'. They have catchphrases—'it's not the cough that carries you off, it's the coffin they carry you off in'—and mock laments:

> Little Willie's dead,
> Jam him in the coffin,
> For you don't get the chance
> Of a funeral often.

Opie says: 'Death, which when they were younger they may have regarded as a frightening and private subject, has now come out into the open. They have found out that it is still a long way off, and these songs are a sign of their emancipation.' Yet I remember saying these and other rhymes, giggling and joking about death, at the same age as when I lay in terror during the night. There is still a lot of room for research on the development of the junior school child. We know now that it is not a 'latent' period. It may seem a stable and quiet period of slow growth, but the roots of adolescence are reaching down and already becoming tangled up with the decaying roots of childhood.

Ruth Griffiths, in *Imagination and Play in Early Childhood*, penetrates more deeply than some of the 'objective observers' of children, for she realizes that the child has a private world not penetrable by grown-ups, and that the imagination cannot always be subjected to psychological tests. She says of death,

the child's ideas are for the most part vague in the extreme and continually changing. He uses the terms he hears others use but they convey much less to him than we usually realize. The idea of death is no exception. The term may have several varied meanings for the same period over a comparatively short period of time. It may mean simply 'absence', it may mean 'injury', the 'dead' person is taken to hospital and made well. In the thoughts of children one may be devoured by a wild animal, but there is no finality about this, for the 'grandmother' may be taken from the 'stomach' of the wolf. They accept images in fairy stories because they are already familiar with images in their own fantasies.

This last is an interesting point. There is a marked tendency today to 'play down' the fairy story in most schools in this country with the exception of those run on Rudolf Steiner principles, where the fairy and folk-tale, myth and legend, is used as an educational method. Children brought up with more realistic stories—with real children and real animals— are not 'fooled' by Jonah and the whale or grandmothers in

wolves' stomachs. They are apt to ask 'how big is a wolf's
stomach?' It would appear that the decline of the fairy tale
has influenced children's attitudes.

Marjorie Hourd, in her fascinating investigations of children's poetry, has this to say in her book *Coming into their Own*:

A child is in constant dread lest something or someone dear
to him should be lost for ever, and many are the charms and
ruses which he employs to ward off the word 'never'. Poetry can
be one of these. Sooner or later he will encounter the idea of
total annihilation . . . This concern with death and destruction
often appears through a child's interest in the internecine warfare
waged in Nature. This crops up frequently in the material here.
It is noteworthy that it occurs in the most direct and full-blooded
way in the work of the children said to be the stable and happy
ones . . . There is a universal dread of disappearance or sudden
appearance, or of things happening to us over which we seem
to have no control. No doubt the desire to overcome such fear
is a strong factor in scientific investigation, as well as in artistic
endeavour.

Seven

ANTIDOTES TO FEAR

Societies which regard the community as all important and the individual as completely subservient to it, 'a cog in the wheel', may condition their members into an acceptance of the death of the individual as something not to be deplored, not to be regarded as a negation of life; something smacking of futility, but as a necessity to the community. Having served the State from birth, through childhood, adolescence, maturity, and as far as possible into old age, the citizen of a totalitarian country dies and makes way for a newer, more efficient citizen. The State lives on.

This positive attitude to the death of the individual is no new thing. It has characterized what Karl Popper calls 'closed societies' since early times, though it can be found in members of more open societies, especially when these are in the dynamic, aspiring phase of their evolution. It may underlie the willingness of human beings to sacrifice their lives for their country, for a cause, and for posterity. The martyr who dies in order that 'the truth may live' is more than likely dying in order that the truth shall live on in a *certain community*, real or imagined. It is unlikely that he would have thrown away his life if, at the moment before the fire under the stake was lighted or the cross was to be erected, certain proof had been offered to him that henceforth there would be no human community either on earth or in heaven for whom anyone could lay down their lives. It is interesting to note that in school today we find both children and adolescents regarding death by martyrdom as 'plain silly'.

Even in democracies where the individual is still held to have some importance as such, the education of the child is becoming more and more concentrated on the group. A

65

child must be socialized, we say. If he does not fit into his peer group he is disturbed, in danger of maladjustment. We would expect this type of education to affect the child's subsequent attitude to death. If he becomes less conscious of his importance as an individual and more aware of his role as a cog in the community wheel, we would expect him to grow up with more positive attitudes to his own death than those of previous more individualistic generations. It would be interesting to attempt to find out if this is so. Widespread research with teams of workers would be involved. All that can be said here is that any positive attitude to death in the sense that it is communally functional is completely negated in all the adolescents I have examined so far by their fears of the death of communities and possibly of the entire human species. One imagines this must be so in all communities today, both open and closed, wherever adolescents have heard of H-bombs, bacterial warfare, and wholesale destruction by other physical and chemical means. Apart from this, modern adolescents who have had 'group activity' in junior and infant school show little desire to die for a cause or indeed to die at all. They do, however, sometimes express the opinion that it is a good thing for older groups to die off in order to make way for the young.

We must remember, too, that so far no community has existed outside of fictional Utopias such as 'Brave New World', in which all the individuals have become standardized. Only by completely controlling heredity as well as the internal and external environments of developing human beings could man possibly eliminate individual differences, and as long as these exist there cannot be a communal attitude to death.

Leaving aside functional aspects of death in relation to communities, what positive attitudes have been found in individuals, and how have these, in turn, influenced the children? Apart from those who believe that death is the gate to eternal life, most of the positive attitudes shown cover up a negative one. When death is regarded as a 'blessed release' in the case of the chronic sick, the very old, the suffering child, and others in agony it is merely that non-existence is better than existence under certain conditions. What has always been striking, however, even in some of these cases, is the tenacious 'will to live' which has been shown. A fortnight before he died, Lord Beaverbrook, asked what he considered the greatest achievement in his life, said, 'That I am alive at eighty-four.' Old men and women who may say they long for death rarely show a real inclination to die. One sometimes hears non-believers in immortality saying that those who have fulfilled themselves in life look upon death with equanimity. But there seems little evidence that old men and women of genius regard death as acceptable. Where are these positive attitudes when the time to die actually comes? Relatives frequently blame doctors and medical research workers for keeping their loved ones alive when in their opinion they would be better dead, but again there is very little evidence to prove that the old and chronically sick object strenuously to this extension of life, unless in severe pain.

Death may be romanticized by some writers and artists who have a positive attitude towards it and feared and hated by others who have negative attitudes. But even the Romantics were not so sure when death actually came near. Keats, who was 'half in love with easeful death' when he wrote the *Ode to the Nightingale,* also had 'fears that I would cease to be' before he had written all that was in his 'teeming brain', and we have no evidence from his friend Severn that Keats welcomed dying at the age of twenty-four from TB. Shelley, with all his talk of suicide and death being 'the veil which those who live call life', did not drown deliberately in the Bay of Spezzia. Blake, who certainly did die with a vision of heaven, nevertheless lived to be seventy, and his positive attitude was a mystical one.

In *Humanist Anthology,* Margaret Knight has two relevant quotations which may be comprehended by older children but are not likely to console, as a child may be just as worried about the fact of his non-existence before birth as after death. In fact, there comes a time when it is just this idea of not being which the adolescent may find so hard to take.

Death is nothing to us and no concern of ours, since our tenure of the mind is mortal. Look back at the eternity that passed before we were born and mark how utterly it counts to us as nothing. This is a mirror that Nature holds up to us in which we may see the time that shall be after we are dead. Is there anything terrifying in the sight—anything depressing—anything that is not more restful than the soundest sleep?

This attitude of Lucretius is reaffirmed by Seneca:

'What,' I say to myself, 'does death so often test me?' Let it do so? I myself have for a long time tested death. 'When?' you ask. 'Before I was born. Death is non-existence.'

Yet such attitudes to death are not positive in the strict sense of the word. If death is to be regarded as functional in the life of the individual, then it must be assumed that if death were to be abolished by scientific discoveries life would lose its purpose. If we had all of time to work in, is it likely that we would be spurred on to produce finished works of art, educational systems, and cities for posterity which might include very few new beings besides ourselves?

First of all, before deciding whether these two functional aspects of death may be regarded as justifying positive attitudes we must ask if they are necessarily true. Would creativity cease if our days were no longer numbered? Are human beings, by nature, procrastinators? This, of course, is bound up with the conception of time, and again we must ask if death is necessarily the means by which we perceive time.

Here I shall refer only to physiological concepts which philosophers sometimes are apt to overlook. What is the source of creative activity in man? Does it not occur in very young children who as yet have very little concept of time— who are apt to think of next week as differing very little from eternity? Children are exploratory and creative from the beginning.

It is highly important that adults should examine their own attitudes and philosophical approaches to death and that teachers in particular should not dismiss the subject as irrelevant. If, for instance in training colleges, the term 'creative activity' were examined at the deepest levels, more teachers might be able to counteract the child's basic fears of death by encouraging explorations at all levels, both practical and intellectual. The idea of 'finishing' jobs, neatly ending a lesson, a composition, packing it all away tidily in desks, and so on, is only too prevalent. No wonder children grow up believing that death is necessary, and at best a tidy end to life, a tidy finish to time.

The Genetic Psychology Monographs 1961 have published a very important article by Herbert Gutman which relates creative activity in man to basic physico-chemical processes in the cell. If this can be shown to be so, presumably if death were abolished creative activity would continue, as it is not merely a psychological process.

In most reported instances the creative process contains an important phase which is organic in character, having all the earmarks of unconscious growth and development, analogous to processes leading to birth. There is almost universal agreement on an involuntary, automatic, and compelling element in the creative process. The process of creation is accompanied by strong emotions not only in artists but also in creative thinkers and inventors, thus involving not only the mental faculties but the totality of the person. The interpretation of the facts cited is inescapable. Creating is more than problem solving, although that is certainly a part of it. It is more than a rational process. It appears *that in the creative process man draws from all his departments* . . .

and

Human creativity is rooted in the general principle of self-duplication. This principle accounts for growth and reproduction as well as for man's creative behaviour. The subjective experiences of men engaged in creation testify to a link between the process of reproduction and creation as has been suspected by various philosophers, psychologists, and biologists . . . the self-duplication of the DNA molecule . . . Seen in this light, creative activity is not merely the result of sublimation of sexual (libidinal) energy as Freud wanted us to believe, but creative energy and sexual energy spring from the same source leading merely to expressions on different levels.

He goes on to point out that there is sufficient energy for both processes. There is no need for the creative to borrow from the sexual and though Freud was right in linking creativity with sexuality he was wrong in making one a derivative of the other. Self-duplication, basic in cell activity, is the root of creativity and it becomes transformed, amplified, and externalized in man's language, music, art, buildings, tools, and machines. If this is so, it is quite certain that death is not necessary in order that man shall create. The kingdom of creativity is within him.

This leaves us with one more positive attitude to examine: death as the ending of one phase and the beginning of another, and in this respect linked to birth. Probably, however, the analogy with birth has been very much over-emphasized by psychologists, philosophers, and religious leaders. Physiologically the two processes have little in common. Birth certainly involves a separation as does death, but what *kind* of separation? The new-born child is not separated from the mother in the same way that the dead are separated, unless indeed the mother dies in childbirth, and then, very quickly, a mother substitute must be found even if only to feed the child with a bottle and keep it warm and sheltered. Again, birth is a continuation into life rather than a beginning— a beginning which took place at conception. There may be the birth trauma and the death agony but they are very different, the one may be influencing the subsequent development *in the flesh*—the other, if it influences any subsequent development, is certainly not examinable.

The one positive attitude to death which has influenced and is still influencing children's attitudes to death is the assertion of immortality, which is so important that it needs a chapter to itself. For if we believe that death is functional in the sense that without it human beings could not enter into a new and different type of living, then, as Blake said, 'We are put on earth a little space' for a certain purpose: he believed 'That we might learn to bear the beams of love'. In this case our philosophy of education will be quite different from those who believe otherwise, though we may agree with them about techniques. Arnaud Reid, in *Philosophy and Education* (1962), says: 'The teachers' attitudes, whatever they are, are important, and it is well to be aware that beliefs make a difference.'

Young children attending Morning Assembly, singing hymns, saying prayers, attending religious instruction lessons

in our State schools, assume that the headmaster believes
that 'Jesus lives' and that our Father is in Heaven when he
sees him open his mouth to sing or pray; they assume that
the class teacher or student telling them the 'Story of Easter'
believes that story in a way in which they do not believe in
Red Riding Hood.

As long as we regard a certain set of beliefs as those which
a child should be taught to hold whether or not his teachers
really believe them we shall certainly influence his attitudes
to life and death. But 'immortality' put across in this way by
unbelievers, half-believers, and doctrinal Christian believers
can hardly lead to genuine positive attitudes.

In the next chapter positive attitudes to death involving
beliefs in immortality will be examined in relation to children's attitudes in this country.

We must not confuse a positive attitude to death with the
free choice of death rather than life in certain circumstances.
Lewis Mumford expresses this very well in *The Conduct of
Life*:

> In the best representatives of the human species God becomes
> manifest in a profound discontent, an impulse towards perfec-
> tion, a purpose severed from self-preservation or self-inflation . . .
> though conditioned to social existence he may withdraw from
> society . . . though tethered to the will to live, a deeper loyalty
> may cause him to elect death.

Many parents must have asked themselves the terrible
question: 'Would you rather see your children live on in any
circumstances than die before they become corrupted?'
Children and adolescents can become indoctrinated with
hate. Is it better for one's sons to die than to be taught to
kill Jews? Some parents preferred to kill themselves and
their children rather than to submit to a fate worse than
death, and this was not always motivated by fear of physical
torture and a worse kind of death. What are people to do
today while there is still danger of corruption? Those who
cannot tell their children that immortality is the reward of
the good life, or indeed give them any certainty, yet may be
able to bring them up with some sort of positive attitude to
death. They may not be able to tell them that the species

will live on or that the universe is eternal, but they may attempt to show them that there is a positive attitude to death though it is a relative one. It is that in some circumstances it may be better to die than to risk becoming less than human. With new techniques of brainwashings and injections unless man spurts forward in moral evolution, this may become a necessary choice. It will be a long time before man learns to control life and death, and it may be long before he learns what is the good life, but young people look forward, and the very effort to achieve is also some sort of a positive answer to death. Even more positive is the desire to know.

These problems, perhaps more specific to our own age than to previous ones where scientific, including psychological, techniques were less developed, are not usually debated by children directly. But adolescents do consider them.

The fostering of the spirit of inquiry is one of the best antidotes to depression arising from the foreknowledge of death. Neither the dogma of immortality nor that of death being the final end is the one most likely to create positive attitudes in the child and adolescent. Nor to the young child is the simple, agnostic 'I don't know' very helpful. But 'No one yet knows' is quite another matter and is in keeping with the natural urge of the exploring child who from babyhood is bent on finding out what life is about.

We all know from observation that the baby who is not 'curious' about his environment is ill. Indeed, lack of the urge to find out by touching, smelling, tasting, seeing, and hearing indicates some sort of handicap. Very early on the child is curious about moving objects and soon he is equally interested in why things stop. We have seen that children first think of death in terms of immobility. In trying to investigate why a butterfly has stopped moving the child may kill it and if given the opportunity may go on with repetitive killings to see if butterflies will always stop if you pinch them hard enough. While this sort of investigation has to be controlled by grown-ups it must be regarded as a positive and healthy attitude to death which occurs before there is any meaning attached to the word. Later on the child will examine dead bodies and probably try.to find out what made them die.

There' is still controversy in educational circles about the age at which children should be allowed to satisfy their curiosity by dissecting dead animals. Susan Isaacs found that some very young children asked 'to see inside' dead animals, and it has been my experience that most junior schoolchildren show both curiosity and sadness when they find a dead animal and the curiosity is dominant. Indeed, it may be a helpful way of overcoming their concern about the dead creature. Most are willing to dissect an animal which they have not known personally—which has been picked up or brought by someone—but the idea of dissecting a classroom pet would be as shocking to the majority as if it were a relative. The trouble is that it is not always advisable on hygienic grounds to encourage the dissecting of animals where the cause of death is unknown. The following account of the dissection of a pet mouse is interesting because the owner started off by wanting to preserve the body and the dissection was a sort of sidetrack:

REPORT FROM STUDENT RE CHILDREN'S ATTITUDE TO DISSECTION

THURSDAY, MARCH 15, 1962, CLASS AGE 9

The children have asked numerous questions about taxidermy due to stuffed birds on the Nature Table. Eric brought his dead pet mouse at lunchtime and wanted to stuff it. I skinned it for him, and gradually more children joined us as they came in for the afternoon. They wanted to see inside the animal, so I began to dissect it, continuing during the afternoon. The children showed great interest, recognizing the kidneys, asking to see the lungs, heart, and brain, which I showed.

The mouse was pregnant. This led to many questions about births, stillbirths, etc. One thought the mother's eyes deteriorated during pregnancy. Some thought the mouse had died because it was pregnant, and general feeling was that pregnancy was a kind of disease. Father's part in conception not referred to.

I felt that those who had watched the process from the beginning were hardly upset, while I saw little sign of this among other children. Tony said he felt slightly sick at first. The overwhelming impression was one of interest.

The numerous questions, discussions, and exchange of knowledge occurred most in mixed groups.

When a boy had a road accident and a girl an appendectomy, the dissection was referred to again. Children wanted to see mouse's appendix. Also all referred to Dr Kildare and thought him real.

Frieda Lawrence described in her memoirs the

minor tragedies of our young lives . . . when our guinea-pigs died of an unexpected early frost, we found them in their pen, stiff and dead. 'Well,' we said, 'if they died of cold maybe if we put them to warm in the oven they will come alive again.' We covered them on a tray with leaves and put them in the oven in the kitchen, but they did not come to life again. They remained dead.

C, aged four, is reported to have loved ladybirds, which she closely watched and observed, noting the two spots on the backs of those which frequented the nursery garden. One day she appeared to have run amok—rushing round the garden stamping ferociously on every ladybird she could find. Asked why she did this, she stated that she wanted to stop them walking about. Looking upon the massacre, she observed with great interest that they couldn't move and they had 'some wings sticking out'. G, aged three, was walking home with his mother when they came across a dead pigeon in the road, which he examined with curiosity and then said, 'What will his mummy say?'

Very young children do not seem to have the 'universal horror of dead bodies' which has been described as common to mankind and other members of the primates. It depends, to some degree, to whom the body belongs and its degree of disintegration or mutilation. Piaget maintains in *Language and Thought of the Child* that curiosity only begins with the child's cognizance of death. Before that time, he asserts, the child finds no elements of surprise in life, and all phenomena are regulated by order—

. . . . till the moment when the child takes cognizance of the difference between life and death. From this moment the idea of death sets the child's curiosity in action, precisely because, if the children also show an intense fascination about the details of painful death, and boys in particular may enjoy inflicting pain on their fellows, this partly springs from curiosity, which is a strong ingredient in all forms of sadism. Grown-ups usually try to prevent children from witnessing bloody spectacles, especially at first hand, but given the chance most boys will evade this control.

In the pre-causal mind, Piaget says, 'every activity is comparable to that of life'. This is certainly true, but it is very difficult to say when a child first becomes aware of the differences between living and not living. If everything that moves and has powers and intentions is, to him, living, what does he actually make of the stationary, the sleeping and the new? Curiosity, in the main, prompts such questions as 'If you kill him (a pigeon) at this little corner of his wing, will he die?' and 'Does it (a caterpillar) know it has got to die if it becomes a butterfly?' (quoted by Piaget), but it is also present in the baby investigating a lump of coal. Of course, to be puzzled about the problem of death, which is really a desire to find out if it has any meaning—'any power of intention'—is very different from puzzling about the differences between the moving and the non-moving ladybirds. C noticed that the ladybirds stopped moving and that when they were squashed their wings stuck out. She did not ask *why* they had stopped—if stopping had any purpose. Perhaps we should distinguish between two kinds of curiosity— one, the sort which notices, explores, investigates for the purpose of adding to one's store of information and experience, and the other, which demands reasons.

Piaget is concerned with the second kind when he says:

We can now see what is the part played by questions about death and accidents. If the child is at this stage puzzled by the problem of death, it is precisely because in his conception of things death is inexplicable. Apart from theological ideas which the child of six or seven has not yet incorporated into his mentality, death is the fortuitous and mysterious phenomenon *par excellence*. And in the questions about plants, animals, and the human body it is those which refer to death which will cause the child to leave behind him the stage of pure finalism, and to acquire the notion of statistical causality or chance.

There may be some confusion in the meaning an adult attaches to the word 'death'. One might argue that the child showing curiosity about dead ducks in the butcher's shop, or killed ladybirds, is not aware that death has taken place.

F

It has been my experience that parents and teachers tend to stifle children's curiosity about death. It is here that the great evasion begins and with it an accentuation of fear of death. We do not know the 'full facts' even about physical death, but we do know some of them. I was impressed by a class of nine-year-olds with whom we were discussing the differences between living and non-living things. They got on to the subject of what happens to the atoms in dead bodies, then to electrons. When it was pointed out that the electrons are still moving in the chemicals of the ashes of the cremated, that they go on 'circling like tiny planets', I watched, like wind passing through a field of corn, looks coming on their faces that can only be described as joy. A boy said 'even in trilobites in the rocks are there these electrons?' And D, who had been terrified of death, looked up eagerly, a smile broadening his face: 'They *could* go on for ever. Bits of me can go on for ever and ever and ever.' I realized then that probably this is the way to help children overcome their fears of death—by telling as much of the truth as we know. Similarly, when the curious child asks what happens to *me* after death or to grandma one need not say 'You or she will disappear for ever' but rather 'People are still trying to find out, just as they are trying to find out what is in space. Probably when you are grown up you'll go on trying to find out too, but the human brain is limited and can't find out everything.'

There is an aspect of curiosity about death which includes a delight in the macabre, and for this reason many teachers and parents try to stifle a child's investigations and even register shocked surprise when he shows great interest in the details of dying. This is particularly common to junior school children, boys especially, and should not be confused with a delight in violence, or with a morbid preoccupation, which may characterize disturbed and psychotic children. After Kennedy's assassination a group of small American boys played out the shooting all the next day, swarming over the neighbours' walls, including mine in the process. 'Hi! Do you know how our President was shot?' shouted the eight-year-old; and, before I could reply, 'Two bullets went into his head and the wound was gaping open, the blood went all over Mrs Kennedy's skirt—did you see it on TV . . . what d'you think'll happen to the assassin? Will someone tear him limb from limb?'

Another child, a girl of nine, also interested in the blood, later on bought a bunch of violets and sent it to the American Embassy. A boy inquired whether they would sew up the wound before the lying-in-state and seemed disappointed when told that the coffin would be closed. A Humanist parent of my acquaintance encourages her children's interest in the corpses of pets and wild animals and tries to be present when they dig them up again after a funeral ceremony. Once they continued until all that was left was a 'lovely lot of white bones'. This can be contrasted with the Duke's recollection in *Thanatos* (Richardson & Toynbee), obviously based on someone's first-hand experience. He is asked when his interest in death began.

Well now, when did it all begin? As a very young child— perhaps five or six years old. I remember stumbling on a dead hedgehog in some rhododendron bushes. The little carcase was alive with maggots, and the stench was both new to me and quite appalling. I ran to my mother and cried for at least an hour on her lap . . . I felt the utmost horror at the physical aspect of death. And then, of course, the Bible powerfully reinforced my feelings, and I haven't even yet recovered from learning that Herod was eaten of worms . . . So it was corruption which first filled me with a horrified fascination, and it was only a good deal later, when a boy died while I was at Eton, that I began to think about extinction.

Another aspect of curiosity about death, which I have not had time to investigate as it was brought to my notice by students recently, is the interest which many children and adolescents show in death notices—not so much epitaphs on tombstones, but the reading of death and 'In Memoriam' notices in newspapers. Some students reported that they had taken great interest in these since about the age of ten and still read them before the 'Births and Marriages'. Asked why they were interested, they said they thought it was the age of the deceased, how the notice was worded, and who the mourners were that really aroused their curiosity. All said they felt a certain degree of identification both with the dead and with the appropriate relative.

All aspects of death arouse children's curiosity, and it is a pity that Camus's words are true. 'Since men cannot cure death, they have made up their minds not to think about it' —and they try to stop children thinking about it. But their dreams, their stories, their art, and their comments on 'Nature' reveal that they are far more interested in death than in God, which is another subject which most grown-ups find embarrassing. Death may be terrible, but it is dramatic, it is real; it happens, and children are naturally curious about it.

This curiosity, when it is verbalized by primary school children is nearly always concentrated on what happens to the body which was once alive, and it appears to be the idea of 'no longer being alive', rather than the prospect of there being no definite signs of an after-life, which worries these young children. A few examples of children's questions and discussions reveal this:

ELIZABETH (aged ten years) (*at home, to mother*—'*out of the blue*', *during washing-up*): 'Do worms really eat dead people? I thought they ate soil?'

'Earthworms do eat soil. I expect they mean maggots.'

'It's better to be cremated, don't you think?'

'Well, I think so.'

'What happens? Are you in a coffin?'

'Yes, the coffin slides into a furnace, out of sight.'

'I wouldn't like that either. How long does it take?'

'Oh, I don't know. A few minutes, that's all. But I shouldn't worry. You won't know anything about it, and we are a long-lived family, you've got heaps of time. What made you suddenly think about it?'

'Nothing. I just wondered. . . . Have I got some clean socks?'

GEOFFREY (aged five and a half years), (*to older brother*): 'Do you go stiff when you die?'

PETER: 'That's why they call them stiffs.'

GEOFFREY: 'Can't you bend at all?'

PETER: 'Course not, you clot. You're dead, aren't you?'

JOHN (*to baby-sitter*): 'How do people die in their sleep? Do they know they're dead?'

'Well, they just go on sleeping.'

'They must know. I won't, will I?'

'Of course not. Only old people die in their sleep.'

Eight

ATTITUDES TO IMMORTALITY

If human life on earth is regarded by adults who are concerned with the upbringing of children as an interlude in eternity, or as a preparation for another existence, death becomes an end and a beginning. Where Christian beliefs are strongly held, and particularly in the more ritualistic sects, the way a man dies is regarded as all-important in determining his future in the next life. Dying and death may become hedged about with taboos and ceremonies, shrouded in a mystery of words, and there is a striking similarity between some forms of Christian funeral rites and those of early societies.

The funeral of Sir Winston Churchill, watched on television by millions of viewers, including children, was a magnificent and impressive spectacle, but a fairly common comment among intellectuals was that the ritual must have been most interesting to social anthropologists. One wondered what an observer from a more highly evolved planet would have made of this 'tribal custom'. Certainly the assertion of immortality was not paramount; it played a very minor part throughout the period of mourning. The Archbishop of Canterbury mentioned once on a TV appearance that Churchill was in paradise, but during the funeral rites one felt that the ceremony was one of farewell only. In the schools some children wrote about Churchill, sometimes voluntarily, but the references to life after death in the schools I visited were negligible.

In the past, among the more significant aspects of attitudes to death was the shadow they threw back over life. Those about to die, even children, must prepare themselves and repent or rejoice according to how they had spent their earthly days. In fact, until this century was well under way

most children in this country were taught that life on earth is
a preparation for eternity. It was regarded by many of them
as another and equally competitive sort of school. The
natural fear of death was aggravated in some cases by the
awful idea that it was the 'Gate to the Unknown'. The word
'unknown' was not used in an agnostic sense, but to denote
one's personal fate.

Although the dread of the unknown may still cling to
adults confronted with the problem of death, it is very rare
to find anyone today whose behaviour pattern on earth is
determined by a firm belief in the possibility of everlasting
torture for the damned. Nor have I discovered in the last
twenty years any child, however rigid his faith, who has been
frightened by hell-fire.

Certainly up to the First World War most teachers would
have supported the inclusion of the Christian teaching on
immortality in terms of heaven in the infant and junior
school, and even up to and including the secondary ages in
many cases. One still finds this implied in some of the agreed
syllabuses. References to an after-life which has a definite
location can be found today during a visit to most infant and
some junior schools, but older boys and girls who draw angels
and spirits floating about in heaven may deny its 'real'
existence when asked where it is. I have found children
referring to heaven and sometimes to hell when asked
directly in the course of casual conversation, but nearly
always in a stereotyped, parrot fashion as something they
repeat rather than learn, and often there is a subtle change
in the tone of voice.

With learning rather than teaching being emphasized in
modern educational methods it is probable that concepts
which the child cannot possibly form by way of any kind of
direct experience and which are foisted on it in a stage of
immaturity will never be truly grasped. Heaven is an abstract, yet it has been taught as if it were concrete. It can
only be realized in fairy-tale fashion by children.

Whenever a conversation with a young child in school
turns on the subject of what happens after death one realizes
how hollow and unconvincing heaven appears to be. I was

talking to an intelligent girl of seven in an infant school in the Harrow area who had been showing me her writings, which were very advanced. She asked, as these children nearly always do, if I would hear her read. She selected a book called *The Creation* from the book corner and started to read. It was Biblical, with contemporary illustrations. After a time she stopped and said: 'What I've been wondering is, how God began. How did he begin?' I asked her how she thought he had begun. 'Like man,' she said, 'he came when a lot of dust got together and formed him!' Another child sitting in the book corner looked somewhat startled—'But he's everlasting.' The first child hesitated, then said: 'I'm not everlasting, am I?' I asked her what she meant. She replied: 'Well, I'll die, won't I?' She seemed a little sad, so I said quickly: 'But not for a very long time, you are only seven.' 'Yes, but I'll die in the end. I'm not everlasting. Won't God finish one day too?' 'Well, what happens when you die.' Like a couple of parrots, this child and the other one chorused: 'You go to Heaven.'

Gesel, in his norms of child development based on observations of American children, refers even to his oldest age group, the sixteen-year-olds, still puzzling over problems of immortality in terms of heaven. In this country today one comes across the belief in immortality as a prolongation of time—eternal life—and only in late adolescence can the more philosophically minded of children, however they are taught, understand such doctrines as that of the eternal moment or eternal recurrence, though reincarnation thought of as a sequence of lives in time appears to be grasped by children in early adolescence.

Whether or not heaven as a location has any meaning for modern children we have to ask if an after-life of any sort has any meaning. There are two very important questions to be answered before examining in more detail the assertion of personal immortality. First, is there any evidence which can be brought forward to support such a belief? If so, we must tell the children what it is. Secondly, even if there is no evidence for such a belief, and it is untrue, or even probably or possibly untrue, is it better to bring up children with such a faith until they are mature enough to face the prospect of personal annihilation?

The first question must be dealt with very briefly here. Believers certainly produce evidence for their beliefs and usually regard this evidence as factual. Although the Apostles' Creed in the Church of England Prayer Book begins 'I believe . . .', it continues as though it were a statement of facts, '. . . was crucified, dead, and buried. He descended into hell; the third day he rose again from the dead, he ascended into heaven. . . .' Generations of churchgoers really believed this, and taught it to their children. That Jesus appeared to the disciples in recognizable form was regarded as a fact as proven as that of two and two making four. And this was also taken as evidence that followers of Christ would likewise rise from the dead.

A similar piece of evidence which is cited by some Christians now, and taught to children in the past, is that Christ was able to raise Lazarus from the dead, though the corpse was putrefying. But even in Church of England schools this sort of evidence, presented as factual in the scientific sense, is not used as often as formerly. The attitude shown in a *Sunday Break* programme on ITV is the more likely one. Adolescents on the screen were asking, 'What is death? What happens when we die?' and the clergyman got out of it nicely by saying, 'The Bible doesn't encourage us to think about it.' But one or two of the young people were not easily deterred, and again a direct question came: 'What is meant by the resurrection of the body?' They were told once more that the teaching of the Bible discourages speculation about death. All that the teenagers got in answer to their very marked interest was that Christianity helps us to believe that 'death is not a full stop'.

The leaders of the Churches and most psychologists appear to be on the same side of the fence in their teachings about death. The religions evade it in almost the same terms as the psychologists. It is unbalanced, immature, neurotic to be unduly concerned about death. Yet not so long ago healthy men and women were so concerned with their 'latter ends' that they believed that one should be preparing for a godly death from the moment one was able to lisp. Some Roman Catholic children now are deliberately taught to meditate on death, nightly, and there is a good deal of evidence from the records that they do, in fact, bring death into the open more often than children not so instructed. I found this particularly in a residential home for Roman Catholic educationally sub-normal boys, when some detailed tests were made on a small group of ten. Heaven was talked about quite naturally as a rather lovely place, but hell was referred to only once by one boy in passing. Purgatory was not mentioned. In Roman Catholic schools for normal children, where tests were done to discover their attitudes to death, both in fantasy and fact, these boys and girls referred to death, the soul, and heaven about three times as frequently as matching groups in undenominational schools.

It is impossible here to make any sort of survey of evidence for survival which comes in the form of reported meetings with the spirits or ghosts of the dead. The Society for Psychical Research examines the evidence for survival, and publishes records of alleged communication between the living and the dead. Spiritualists deliberately try to get into touch with the departed, many of whom appear to be strangely interested in the trivia of earthly life.

On almost another plane are some of the mystics and the pantheists, who think of survival of bodily death in terms of being united to the 'Divine Ground', one with God or with Nature. The sort of evidence these people produce is what they regard as undeniable first-hand experience.

Parents and teachers may subscribe to one or other of these beliefs in some form, and if so will influence their children's attitudes to death either directly or indirectly.

Sylvia Anthony thinks that:

Religion, wherever it has a hold, performs a function. The cure is not, though to outsiders it may seem, worse than the disease . . . The Calvinist and the Catholic braved the hell they vividly imagined, through insistence on justification by faith and through grace.

And

Every form of religion, in the sight of its adherents, offers more, in the relief of distress about the ending of the individual life, than it takes away in hope and blind security. Any form of religion sincerely held by the adults of a group to which a child belongs may provide that child with an 'escape into reality' when he spontaneously turns to it. Such escapes are often valuable and sometimes critical and essential stages in the child's mental adjustment.

This brings us to the next question. How far is it justifiable to bring up children on myths and on beliefs no longer held by the adults who are concerned with him? We have already discussed the dilemma of Humanist parents whose children must submit to assemblies and religious instruction in State schools and usually to compulsory chapel in preparatory and public schools, unless they risk singling out a child for special treatment. Progressive schools are becoming rarer and extremely expensive, as they have no subsidy. Yet so far, the move to abolish compulsory religion in schools has got no further than the move to abolish corporal punishment. Is there any connection?

There are parents and teachers, unbelievers themselves, who nevertheless think that children 'need religion'. Some go as far as sending their children to Church and Sunday school, occasionally going there themselves to keep up appearances before their children. Thus the parents go on silently accepting the prospect of coming annihilation, while the children believe in heaven or some other place of eternal life. Does this help? More research is needed into this, together with more investigations on the place of myth and fairy tale in education.

Many observers have found that fear of death is even more pronounced in children with a religious upbringing, but unless there has been deep analysis it may be difficult to tell how much fear there is in those who do not show it. Alexander and Adlerstein, in various psychological journals, record their findings of investigations into death anxiety in matching groups of religious and non-religious students. 'The most general conclusion called for by this set of findings is that death anxiety, as we measured it in this particular sample, is by no means dissipated by a religious approach to life.' They go on to say that earlier memories of death are recalled more easily by the religious, that there is more anxiety concerning one's own death in the religious, whereas in the non-religious 'the defence is repression'.

It appears to be true today that most parents and teachers are never confronted with the question: 'What happens after death?' I have not come across it once, directly, in my experience of children, and only a few parents have reported that their children show overt concern with the after-life, though fear of dying and death is very evident. Bereavement now being relatively uncommon in the period after the Second World War, children rarely have to grieve for the death of any but the very old. A small group of university students at a party recalled clearly their attitudes to death, all but one of them having been brought up with no religion, and all born during the early years of the War. They said even had they been taught to believe in an after-life they did not think their attitudes would have been altered very much. Four of them are quoted below.

S.—I remember clearly putting two ink-blots on the wall, one representing my death and the other the death of my mother. I was about seven. I did not even think of putting a third blot to represent the death of my father. I suppose I was in the Oedipus phase. The blots affected me emotionally every time I looked at them, but I can't say if they represented extinction.

L.—When I was seven I was terrified of my own death and said to my mother: 'I don't mind if you die, but I won't die, will I?' My mother was not in the least offended, and I remember being rather surprised.

M.—My friend, aged ten, was convinced that she was going to die tomorrow, so went cycling round to see all she could first. I was brought up as a Catholic and thought it rather a mistake.

T.—I was nearly drowned when I was nine and I remember when we were semi-conscious my friend saying: 'You *will* say goodbye to mummy, won't you?'

One of them added that when she was looking after a child of four he asked, 'Why do people die?' and then, 'If I die when I'm on my tricycle it will go to heaven with me, won't it?' This is typical of children's fears about death. (They dread leaving this life, and there is not much evidence that as far as they are concerned notions of eternal bliss in a spirit world help very much. So perhaps it is true to say that for the majority of children whether their parents are believers or unbelievers is neither here nor there when it comes to fear of their own death. But it may be quite another matter when children are worried about the deaths of relatives and friends. Does it help to believe that the dead parent is still 'alive' somewhere else and has not disappeared for ever? All one can say is that it may help some children at a certain age, and that even in the same family a wise parent may alter the dose of truth to suit the individual child concerned even if the parent himself is an agnostic or an atheist.)

Leslie Mumford, in *The Conduct of Life*, reports the attitude of parents towards their five-year-old when the baby Billy died at five months. 'With Truth as our guiding goal' they helped the older brother to accept the fact of his disappearance. This would have been a more difficult task had the child been older than five. Even children who have been brought up with a positive approach to death in religious upbringing may be shattered by the death of a parent. Thus D, aged twenty-six, recalls her reaction to the news of her father being killed in the War when she was five, the same age as Billy's brother who had been brought up without faith. 'I shouted at God all night. I just couldn't believe that he had let them kill my father. I loathed him for it.' Richard Steele remembers 'beating on his father's coffin' in a blind rage when he was four, and Crabbe in 1754 writes on the death of a sister:

> But it was misery stung me in the day
> Death of an infant sister made his prey,
> For then first met and moved my early fears
> A father's terrors and a mother's tears.
> Though greater anguish I have since endured,
> Some healed in part, some never to be cured,
> Yet there was something in that first born ill
> So new, so strange, that memory feels it still.

'There is yet another fear that may darken the mind in childhood and haunt the day—the dread and fear of death,' writes Walter de la Mare in *Early One Morning*. It seems that no teachings concerning immortality mitigate the dread of death when it occurs in childhood. There may be a terror associated with the very idea of everlasting life. This is very well expressed by Neville Cardus, the cricketer, in his autobiography:

Terror overwhelmed me one day when I read in a newspaper that according to a German scientist named Professor Falb the end of the world would take place on November 13th, 1899. Through all my infancy the idea of eternity has appalled me. I would lie in bed at night trying to imagine us all going on for ever and ever. I saw a small compressed space remote in the sky, a trap from which there was no escape. 'For ever and ever and ever and ever and ever and ever,' I would murmur to myself in the dark, thinking hard on the word 'ever' until my mind became a piercing tunnel of terror reaching on without end. But Professor Falb and the Last Day were forgotten as the years went by.

On the other hand, F. R. Leavis, in *The Common Pursuit*, quotes Every in the chapter on 'The Logic of Christian Discrimination', who suggests that it is difficult to see a purpose in life at a time when progress is no longer expected and there is no faith in a better life:

The younger poets who came to light in 1937–42, such voices as Dylan Thomas, David Gascoyne, Alex Comfort, and Sidney Keyes, have never suffered from any illusions about the future of our civilization. For them the urgent problem is the imminence of death, the need of some significance that can be attached to dying in a world where there is no common belief in immortality.

What evidence is there that the belief in immortality is no longer widespread? In December 1947 the British Institute of Public Opinion asked a sample from the whole of Britain: 'Do you believe in a life after death?' The results are given below:

Yes	*No*	*No Opinion*
49%	33%	18%

Forty-three per cent of men believed and 55 per cent of women. Among the denominations the results were:

	%
Spiritualists	90
Roman Catholics	62
Church of England	46
Jews	32

One wonders what the other 10 per cent of the Spiritualists believe. Where are the Spirits?

The 49 per cent who believed in an after-life were asked what it was like; 13 per cent did not know. Of the rest:

3% gave miscellaneous replies.

19% said the spirit lives on.

4% said one went to heaven or hell according to the life one had lived on earth.

3% believed in reincarnation.

3% believed in Paradise.

2% said one went to life on a higher plane.

2% said the after-life was similar to life on earth.

In 1950 a survey was made about belief in ghosts; only 8 per cent men and 12 per cent women affirmed a belief in them.

G. Gorer in 1955 produced an interesting analysis entitled *Exploring English Character*. He found that beliefs in the after-life could be divided into the following ten categories:

(1) Scriptural Heaven and Hell and/or Purgatory. Direct references to the Bible and/or Judgment (the good rewarded, the bad punished).

(2) Scriptural Heaven (references to God, Jesus, the holy family, but no references to Judgment or punishment for the wicked).

(3) After-life not like Scriptural Heaven (explicit disbelief in angels, harps, etc).

(4) Beauty, Rest, Peace, etc (stated positively, no reference to God).

(5) Absence of evil, pain, worry, inequality, etc (stated negatively: no reference to God).

(6) Rejoining loved ones.

(7) Watching over loved ones.

(8) Like this life.

(9) Reincarnation.

(10) Life on another planet.

It is interesting to note that the mystical experience of union with the divine seems to be missing.

Freud asks:

How did primitive men arrive at the peculiar dualistic views on which the animistic system is based? It is supposed that they did so by observing the phenomenon of sleep (including dreams) and of death, which so much resembles it, and by attempting to explain those states, which are of such close concern to everyone. The chief starting-point of this theorizing *must have been the problem of death. What primitive man regarded as the natural theory was the indefinite prolongation of life—immortality. The idea of death was only accepted late, and with hesitancy. Even for us it is lacking in control and has no clear connotation.*

If we were to try to introduce quite different attitudes towards life and death, time and eternity, into our schools in place of what goes for religious education today, if we deliberately fostered the intuitive and abandoned our competitive 'race for the goal' type of schooling, it would alter completely our culture. The Christian religion is time-conscious, humanity-centred, based on a birth and a death and a resurrection which was actually timed. The new interpreters of 'a religion without God' may recommend that we 'learn to swim in the infinite', but this will be meaningless to a child below the age of mid-adolescence.

Nine

FEAR OF DEATH

It is, of course, impossible to separate positive and negative attitudes to death. Positive attitudes which suggest that death is meaningful include all those which stem from beliefs in an after-life, those which find a social meaning in death, and those which are simply exploratory. Curiosity, which has been described in a previous chapter as a positive attitude, may end in a negative one of fear as the child investigates the dead, maggot-ridden bodies of animals or discovers that the dead mother will never return. Fear itself, provided it is not excessive, may give rise to a more positive approach. If fear of death were entirely removed, personal and mass suicides might increase, and in this sense it acts as a preventative. Indeed, in some cases of congenital brain damage where an individual grows up without fear he has to be protected from self-destruction. It also has been suggested in previous chapters that many who regard death as functional would argue that fear of death may result in an acceleration of human endeavours, in a desire for maximum achievement, in the creation of 'immortal works of art', and it may underlie man's urge to leave children behind him. But fear may also stimulate man to experiment on ways of getting rid of death and may spur him on to replace dying organs of the body and certainly to postpone most people's deaths until old age. Fear, of course, is a complex and negative emotion, and the purpose of this chapter is to consider it mainly as it occurs in children. We must distinguish between fears of two distinct events—that of dying and that of death.

Fear of the act of dying, apart from its being a prelude to death, is mainly physical and is often associated with terror of a particular *way* of dying. Children are very prone to this

kind of fear, which may reveal itself in dreams and nightmares. The source of such fears may lie in books, newspapers,
and magazines read by children, in overheard conversations
of grown-ups, in television and radio programmes, in stories
told by other children, and occasionally when the act of
dying is observed in human or animal and in bereavement.
Certain phrases may strike absolute terror into a child
whether he reads or hears of them. Such a one is 'the death
agony', which for long years he may believe to accompany
all forms of dying.

This term 'agony' was used extensively in describing the
final days of the late Pope John. The 'death rattle' made me
cold with horror when as a child of six or seven I first heard
of it. The child imagines these phenomena to be unspeak-
ably terrible. Children brought up to be familiar with
'Christ's agony on the Cross' and to repeat such phrases as
'By thy agony and bloody sweat' may become even more
terrified, though the more resilient ones will learn to defend
themselves from the onslaught of these piercing words. Today fear of death from lingering disease is less likely to be
present than fear of death by violence, though some aspects
of violent death have recurred in children's dreams as long
as these have been recorded. Dying by any form of suffoca-
tion arouses terror and is common in nightmares. Charlotte
Yonge refers to 'one most gratuitous alarm recurring every
night—of being smothered like the Princes in the Tower or
blown up with gunpowder. In the daylight I knew it was
nonsense. I would have spoken of it to no one, but the fears
at night always came back.'

A particular fear in childhood, more so than in later life,
is of sudden death. Not only does this appear to be a
terrible manner of dying but it makes life itself appear so
entirely unstable. Children of junior school age appear to
be peculiarly afraid of sudden death although they may tell
each other that it is better 'you don't know it's coming'—
'it's over before you realize it'. But when these children are
older and are willing to relate their childhood fears that of
sudden death is often among them. Sometimes their terror of
sudden death is mingled with fear of being deprived of a

longed-for treat. 'I was absolutely terrified that I might die
suddenly before tomorrow, when we were going to the sea-
side. I prayed "just let me live for a few days more until I've
enjoyed some bathes and the boat. It won't be so bad then."'
(B, aged nine.) Others have wanted to live until their birthdays, or Christmas, or until a friend has returned.

One wonders what sort of nightmares concerning sickness
and dying were invoked by children who received such
books as *The Juvenile Keepsake* for their birthdays. This little
volume of poems selected by James Murray and published
in 1850 contains the famous gem by Watts:

> Have you not heard what dreadful plagues
> are threatened by the Lord,
> To him that breaks his father's law,
> Or mocks his mother's word?
>
> What heavy guilt upon him lies!
> How cursed is his name!
>
> The ravens shall pick out his eyes
> And eagles eat the same.

The last two lines must surely have accentuated another of
the commoner fears associated with certain methods of
dying, one which strangely persists today in children even in
urban areas—that of being devoured by wild animals or
otherwise mutilated and killed by them. It comes in nightmares, dreams, and fantasies so often that it must be regarded as archetypal. Being eaten, of course, has a ritualistic
meaning, but here we are concerned with it only as it is
associated with fear. But the child, who in play threatens to
'eat you all up', is probably revealing a complicated emotional urge, partly ambivalent. The threat to devour one
may also include a talion theme, or the child may be trying
to defend himself against his own dread of being eaten.

A boy as old as nine repeatedly had nightmares that wild
animals were coming upstairs to kill him. In his case the fear
was rooted in an actual earlier experience—when he was a
young child in Africa saved from a snake. The phrase 'died
of a broken heart', probably heard in a fairy story, so captured the imagination of my son that he woke up screaming

at the age of six, shouting that his heart had cracked and he was dying.

I myself particularly dreaded dying by poisoning because someone had told me that when Socrates drank the hemlock the poison gradually mounted up from his legs until it reached his heart, and at that moment he fell dead.

Children still dread dying by falling from heights, and in spite of the exploits of astronauts, parachutists, and the like, still argue as to whether one is 'dead before one reaches the bottom'. Coming up three times before drowning, during which time the whole of one's past life is relived, is another terrifying myth associated with this particular way of dying. But the chief fear of the grown-up and child alike is probably that of intense pain. Very often children who have watched animals die have an exaggerated idea of the amount of pain which may be associated with dying today. Children who express such fears of dying in pain can be consoled by information about pain-killing drugs, and even in the case of deaths from accidents there is less likelihood of prolonged pain than there used to be. Nevertheless, children from an early age do show their awareness of agony in their play and drama, in writings and paintings. Playing at killings, they may writhe on the floor, scream, and generally 'act out' what they believe to be the accompaniments of violent death. It is interesting to note that in these games no one comes to relieve the sufferer, yet in hospital play, which is now a great feature of free activity periods in infant schools, little dressed-up nurses and doctors are armed with hypodermics, and no one is allowed to lie in pain. Nor in hospital play have I ever witnessed a death, except with nursery children, who regard it as reversible. People have ghastly illnesses, legs and arms amputated, but they survive. The very same children may move from one sort of game to the other. Confronted with actual dying in pain, they nearly always react with horror even if they cover this up when they are older.

But it would be dangerous to eliminate fear of pain altogether. It is rightly dreaded by human beings as it is able to negate not only action but thought itself. Anyone who has suffered really intense pain knows this. To inflict death on another is something which children quickly accept as being 'wrong' unless, unfortunately, they are brought up to believe that it is acceptable in case of war, or judicially. In our society they are also taught that death by torture is the most reprehensible type of killing.

Other fears associated with the act of dying which children, in particular, dread are the changes in the familar physiological functions, particularly the deterioration in responses and the onset of darkness. The latter used to occur frequently in Victorian fiction—'why is it growing so dark, dear mamma, when it is still morning?' Coldness, too, is another of the dreads, and though not so common now that corpse-touching has gone out of fashion children may be aware of it when they first come across phrases such as 'cold and dead' in folk-songs. It was found by Stanley Hall in an article in the *American Journal of Psychology* published in 1915 that children in the earlier part of the century did associate death with coldness.

From Scott's 256 cases and my own 299 returns to questionnaires it appears that the first impression of death often comes from a sensation of coldness on touching the face or hands of a corpse of a relative and the reaction is a nervous start at the contrast with the warmth which cuddling and hugging are wont to bring.

A programme on TV in the early spring of 1962 appeared to reveal that when actually faced with dying very few show fear of death, but there are several points to note here. Firstly, those that report they were not afraid when faced with imminent death, did not, in fact, die. The relief of escape from almost certain death may have been so great that it blotted out memories of fear. Secondly, those who faced death in the acute stage of disease were obviously very ill, possibly doped, or, if not, were certainly not in a state of vigour. Death may seem the lesser of two evils to those experiencing great pain or great fatigue. Doctors and nurses as well as clergymen often report that they have never seen anyone really afraid to die except by execution or other forms of violence, but how can they tell? Most people do not want their relatives to remember them going out in a state of terror.

W. H. Davies, in *The Autobiography of a Super-Tramp*, 1908, says:

Now I have heard a great deal of dying men having a foresight of things to be, but I confess that I was never more calm in all my life than at this moment when death seemed so certain. I did not for one instant believe or expect that these eyes would again open to the light, after I had been in this low vital condition deadened and darkened for over two hours while my body was being cut and sawn like so much wood or stone. And yet I felt no terror of death. I had been taken in a sleigh from the station to the hospital, over a mile or more of snow, and the one thought that worried me most, when I was supposed to be face to face with death, was whether the town lay north, south, east, or west from the hospital, and this I believe was the last question I asked.

But Davies did not die, and on his own showing he was in a very low state of vitality.

Fear of death itself is equally complicated, and one, or all, of the following seven aspects may be involved.

The first is fear of non-existence, which has already been briefly referred to. Blankness, nothingness is not easy to contemplate, and Freud and others have stated that it is totally unacceptable to human thought. 'It is indeed impossible to imagine our own death; and whenever we attempt to do so we can perceive that we are, in fact, still present as spectators. Hence the psycho-analytic school could venture on the assertion that at bottom no one believes in his own death.'

Psychologists who tend to regard fear of death and/or preoccupation with it as at best neurotic often add a faint reproof for those of us who confess our sins openly in this respect. We are the egocentric ones, immature, what former teachers would have called selfish. Alexander and Adlerstein, in 'Studies in the Psychology of Death', conclude: 'It becomes more and more apparent from the increased volume of clinical material that death is a problem which man does not find easy to handle. In some instances fear of death is a primary symptom of pathology, in others general inability to handle life's problems.'

Flugel found that in those who fear death the self-regarding sentiment is excessive, and it should be replaced by other emotions.

If it is the self-regarding who strongly object to the idea of non-existence, as far as my observations go the majority of these people have every right to admire themselves. They are usually men and women of great ability, lovers of life, positive rather than negative in their attitudes. It is most marked in children; the ones who show most fear of death are the highly intelligent and gifted, those in whom 'the gale of life blows high'. The more vital our existence, the more infuriating is the prospect of non-existence. The vigorous, virile, creative Picasso loathes the prospect of death.

The second aspect of fear of death is uncommon in children and most common in the middle-aged. It is then that death seems to negate life and one is struck by the futility of all one's achievements. Death appears to make life so temporary that it is meaningless. The passing of time is accelerated. No sooner is it midsummer than Christmas approaches, and the years seem to get out of control, speeding down hill to death like a car with no brakes. This was well-expressed by a gifted, healthy boy of nine whose responses to the question 'What do you think a boy would wish for if he were given three wishes?' were tape-recorded: 'He would wish never to die because he is so lively he enjoys life so much. He loves getting up in the morning and having his breakfast and going to school, and his next wish would be that none of his family would ever die, and actually his third wish would be that no one need die.'

Of twenty children of this age all said to be 'normal', fourteen included among their wishes one referring to the desire to 'live for ever'. Repeated with a matching group of eleven-year-olds, there were twelve children who expressed this wish.

At a party of forty grown-ups in casual conversation nearly all said they would like to live for ever in some way and that they hated the idea of death whenever they thought of it; and a questionnaire given to students in 1960 revealed that though they were not excessively preoccupied with thoughts of death when they did think of it they feared it.

Not long ago education authorities, writers in the Press, parents, teachers, and 'the man in the street' were shocked to hear of a certain school which had been holding 'death lessons'. The outcry was interesting because it revealed a deep emotional fear of death. The children apparently were asked to pretend they were dead—it was a rehearsal of death. One would have liked the opportunity to examine the reactions of the children objectively. As such, though it may be 'cranky', a death lesson surely may do no more harm than many other kinds of lessons. It cannot, however, be a real rehearsal, but perhaps we should bring death out into the open and train children in some way to face up to the inevitable.

With more research on old age we may find that to 'practise' death is as beneficial as to rehearse birth. While mothers-to-be are doing exercises and controlling their breathing ready to give birth perhaps we shall have similar classes for the aged so that 'natural death' will be as painless as natural childbirth. I, for one, would be pleased to attend. The best way to overcome fear of the unknown is to make it more known. I have never yet read a really good account of what one ought to expect.

To children, of course, many things in life are still in the future, unknown, unexperienced. Yet we believe in preparing them in some way for sexual life and telling them the facts. How far should we tell them about death when it is normally still far off? One school, in order to try to avert fear of cancer, teaches the older secondary school children about the biology and physiology of malignant growths. No fear was apparent—only interest and a desire to know enough about it to help people with early symptoms. It is a debatable point how much to tell a child other than answering his direct questions, but not one that we should dismiss out-of-hand.

The fifth aspect of the fear of death will be dealt with in another chapter as it is basic in children. This is the dread of separation. In young children separation and death are almost synonymous and both are total. The small child separated from mother, home, beloved toys, experiences a sort of death. The most poignant aspect of death to the majority of adults, except the extremely old whose friends and relatives have predeceased them, is separation from loved ones and even from a certain environment.

There remains one other major fear experienced by adherents to religions which teach that what happens in the after-life is determined by one's way of life on earth. All I need add to what I have already said is that this fear still exists in some children today, though it is fast fading out as doctrines of hell fire and other forms of eternal punishment are played down.

A curious, but common variant of fear of death in children is their wishing this fear on to adults, particularly when these adults are attempting to discipline them. Usually in fantasy, rarely in fact, the child will use the parent's dread of the death of the child as a revenge for punishment or anger. Many children imagine their own death-bed scenes with terrified and remorseful adults repenting, too late, of having been angry with the child. Children rarely actually threaten to kill themselves or to 'run away and never come back', thus showing their strong belief that the worst that can happen to their parents is loss of their offspring.

Ten

FEAR OF SEPARATION

Perhaps the most persistent of fears associated with death is that of separation—and the one which is most likely to be basic, independent of cultural, religious, or social background. We find it present in early man and in primitive societies today, even where the individual is merged into the tribe and hardly exists in his own right. Burial customs and rituals reveal both a terror of the dead and a desire to be rid of them for ever, and at the same time a terror of separation, of the unknown, and a desire to negate death by assuming that something of the deceased lives on.

In children dread of separation seems to be basic. Freud regards the young child's idea of death as equivalent to disappearance or going on a journey, and indeed separation from the mother is a death to a young baby. The mother who returns again after a short absence of a day or two may indeed be a different person to the child she has left, and the relationship he builds up the second time may be to a second mother, the first having 'died'.

I remember having to leave my daughter for four days when she was about nine months old, to be greeted on my return by a look of such blankness that I felt it as a manifestation of non-existence. At an older age—about fourteen months—I was obliged to leave my son for almost a week and was met by the same stare of non-recognition. Bowlby's findings in *Child Care and the Growth of Love* have been confirmed many times by parents. It may not be quite disastrous to leave a baby in its first two years for a short time, but I am inclined to think that once the separation has become absolute to the child, and the mother has 'disappeared', it is a new mother, a resurrected one perhaps, to whom attachment is newly made. Shelley is the only person reported to have questioned babies in their prams about life and death. We can make certain tests on them, but so far there is no direct method of finding out what separation actually means to them except in terms of symptoms.

Sylvia Anthony states that a child 'cannot develop the concept of death' until it has reached the 'why' stage, as 'why' is concerned with the functioning of things and no simple 'thing' meaning can be attached to death. But a very young child may experience separation and feel it to be an eternal one.

Paul, aged two, staying at his grandmother's, barely speaking, was inconsolable when separated from his 'hum', a rolled-up cloth which he took to bed every night. Luke, also two, consoled himself with a formula, 'back soon', whenever anyone in the family or even their friends departed through the front door. The earliest records I have of children vocalizing their fears of separation by death occur at the ages of three to four. During the flying bomb and rocket raids on London in 1945 Mary, aged three years five months, during the week sat up in bed and said: 'Will I be killed tonight?'—'No.' 'Will you be killed tonight?'— 'No.' And then went into a peaceful sleep until morning. She had come from New Zealand and twice daily had done lifeboat drill, so her concept of death was probably crystallized early.

In the nursery school, aged four, a boy painted a picture of a boy 'sinking' himself because his mother had died. John, in one of the infant schools I have investigated, aged four, was distressed because the newt on the Nature table had a wound. 'Will it die and have to be buried so that we'll never see it any more?' The other children seemed indifferent. Even very young children vary from day to day in their attitudes. The same boy who felt that the death of a mother could not be faced, a few days later, when going to bed, remarked calmly: 'When I'm lying dying in my bed I shall put Teddy on the chair by my side ready for the next boy.'

Separation, of course, may be welcomed temporarily by young children, and their ambivalent attitudes to relations

is shown by many close observers of nursery children such as
Susan Isaacs. Sometimes death wishes are overtly expressed
as in her instance: 'If you would go away I could cut my hair
as I liked.' Then there is the threat to kill Mrs I and Miss B
—'Yes, we don't mind being alone, do we?'

Children will chop up their grandmothers in the rages of
imagination, push their brothers down the lavatory and pull
the chain so that they can vanish like faeces.

What Sylvia Anthony calls dread of 'sorrowful separation' lies at the root of many beliefs in an after-life. It is the
parting from the individual with all his idiosyncrasies, his
daily routines and his bodily shape, which makes loss so
poignant in our individualistic culture. This, too, lies behind the dread of one's own death—the non-existence of the
individual, the disintegration of the body which has enjoyed 'the wild joys of living'. In fact, separation *from* one's
body is not regarded now as a happy event even by the
religious. Those tribes and ancient civilizations which mani-
fested this type of sadness in their funeral and burial rituals,
in embalming, in ancestor worship and communing with the
dead, have much in common with children and with those
who strongly dislike the idea of death of the individual.
Even fear of the dead, ghosts, and malevolent spirits is a
manifestation of the same attitudes to sorrowful separation.

To a child who has become mature enough to understand
the meaning of time the first shock caused by the death of a
loved one will be the realization that this sort of separation
differs not only in degree but also in kind from any formerly
experienced. The child may remember how he missed his
mother while she was in hospital, or having a baby, or away
visiting, and death will also include this sort of loss. As it
was when she was away, he will not be able to see or talk to
her, share the day-to-day experiences of home and school.
But the separation was not absolute and permanent. He
could write, receive postcards, perhaps telephone. Other
people whom he trusted might see her and report back.

At first he may find it hard to believe that he will be
separated for the whole of the rest of his life. Moreover, the
real nature of this separation only dawns on him when his

first grief is over. Time, which he may have been told 'heals all things', will separate him in an even more absolute sense, for his mother will remain the same in memory but he will grow and develop. The fourteen-year-old boy who lost his mother at six will have known her only as the mother of an infant. Children told stories of being re-united in the after-life will often feel embarrassed at the idea of meeting parents who died when they were smaller. Separation from siblings likewise will be made absolute by time whatever myth or belief a child has been given. A child of seven whose brother died at one year when he himself was four said: 'Andrew won't go on growing in heaven, will he? Could he get older than me! When I go to Jesus I won't know him and he'll wonder who I am.'

On rare occasions death of others is welcomed by children. Separation from a hated grandmother or even a parent may be the end of an intolerable situation, but however strongly the child has wished for this death when it actually happens intense guilt feelings occur along with the sense of relief. Even where children have been physically afraid of a drunken father the total removal of him in death is an even more frightening experience and one for which they may hold themselves responsible.

Reluctance to accept the disappearance of the individual at death underlies a great many myths, superstitions, and beliefs about the departed. The Mass of the Angels was said for the Kennedy baby and there are still children brought up to believe that the body is transformed into an incorruptible one.

Children today are more inclined to refer to ghosts than angels, often in a jocular fashion. It is doubtful whether one would find an Etonian of Shelley's mentality today who would write:

> While yet a boy I sought for ghosts, and sped
> Through many a listening chamber, cave and ruin
> And starlight wood, with fearful steps pursuing
> Hopes of high talk with the departed dead.

Ghosts, spirits, and the dead in remembered forms still haunt our dreams and though separation may be absolute in the daytime the departed may return at night, sometimes to terrify us, sometimes to make awaking to reality a bitter experience. Children, too, may be re-united to their dead in dreams and nightmares, just as they may also in dreams kill their dearest relatives. Psychoanalysis has concentrated on the dream as revealing the causes of disturbance. Maybe the very dream of itself can set up a new sorrow in the child, who wakes up to find that it is not true and that the mother who appeared in the sleep of the night isn't really alive.

Children's imaginary compositions both in writing and art, and their play, may include supernatural spirits. In a nursery school playground in London a group of boys were chasing another group with wild cries. Thinking this was the usual 'Cops and Robbers', I asked the nearest boy if they had captured anyone yet. 'Course not,' he said, 'them's ghosts. You can't catch ghosts.' Asked what a ghost was, another bright four-year-old replied: 'It's something that's not really.'

The belief that the dead exist in some sort of bodily form usually resembling the human dies hard. Even a shadowy body seems to be regarded as better than none. Such beliefs range from the grey ghosts to the beings who still appear to indulge in the pleasures of earthly life, albeit invisibly. The Society for Psychical Research, investigating extra-sensory perceptions, has as yet submitted no convincing evidence that communication between the dead and the living may occur by this means. The Spiritualists still hold their seances and 'mediums' assert that they are in contact with the departed, who appear to reject separation from the living and even try to live as if on earth.

A belief in immortality which refuses to accept the bodily separation of the dead from the living even if the contact of the two is postponed to a 'Day of Resurrection' presupposes that there is survival of recognizable individuals in a space–time continuum against a clearly distinguishable background. When Paul cried 'who will deliver me from the body of this death' he welcomed the eventual separation of his earthly body from his soul, which would be resurrected in a heavenly body. Nevertheless, he did not regard the new body as wholly different from the old one: 'This mortal must put on immortality . . . we are sewn in corruption, we shall be raised in incorruption.' It is difficult now for agnostics to realize what this meant and still means to some Christians and doubly difficult to know what it means to the Christian child in our scientific society today.

Pantheistic theories in which the individual at death is separated from all individuals but is made one with Nature, or mystical ones where he is united with the Divine ground in which all others will also find union, are easier, it seems, for children to understand. The children who were thrilled to think that their dead bodies finally disintegrated into molecules and maybe atoms and electrons before they entered into the composition of other compounds are more likely to grasp theories of reincarnation and pantheism than orthodox Christianity, which is exceedingly difficult conceptually. Indeed, observations of children who have not been brought up in any definite faith do show that their first attempts at explanation of what happens at death tend to be naturalistic and closer to 'earth myths' of rebirth than to the Christian belief in immortality. With regard to the fear of separation there is little to show that the type of reunion taught by the traditionalists of the Christian religion is acceptable as a means of solace, and the new 'image of God' which Robinson and others are trying to introduce is quite beyond many adolescents.

Whatever ideas young children may have of death they normally associate separation from loved ones with sadness. When word association tests were tried out it was found that among three matching classes of seven-year-olds only five brought in death in connection with the word 'sad', but when the word was prefixed by *very* forty-five children out of ninety-one referred to death. Mother's death was most frequent, followed by siblings and then pets. No one mentioned father, but this does not necessarily imply that his death is dreaded less. It may be that young children feel that the father is stronger, more remote, less likely to disappear.

Eleven

BEREAVEMENT

If the problem of answering a child's direct questions about death is fraught with difficulties, it becomes even more formidable if there has been bereavement. Indeed, a number of children react to personal bereavement by withdrawal. The problem of bereavement is much more likely to come up in the home than in the school, though now that teachers are concerned with the education of the whole child and have access to personal and family records in case of difficulty it may be the school that finally brings the problem to light and helps to solve it.

With very young children the term 'bereavement' will cover all losses of persons and objects, even temporary ones. In his papers on 'Grief and Mourning in Infancy and Early Childhood' and 'Separation Anxiety' John Bowlby asserts that 'the responses of infants to loss of objects do not differ from those of adults, and those responses are grief and mourning'.

In a more recent paper in the *International Journal of Psychoanalysis* (1961) Bowlby refers to a type of mourning which man may share with some of the lower animals and seems to be biologically rooted, though this is also 'specific to man', and another type which he calls pathological and which manifests itself in 'persistent seeking for the lost object'.

All research workers are agreed that in the early years the most severe type of bereavement is mother loss, and unless dealt with by adequate mother substitution it may lead to pathological changes in personality development. Patterns of adult mourning have changed, but even if blinds are not drawn or black worn children detect grief very quickly and react to it. We do not yet know, though research is going on all the time, quite what the effects of a father's sorrow may be on the baby even if there is a mother substitute, for 'fathers are parents too'. Older children will respond by grief, but their reactions may include guilt feelings.

Two mothers reported the following children's overt expressions of guilt:

'I should have given Tim my tricycle. He wanted it, Mummy. Then he wouldn't have died, would he?' said a six-year-old.

'Is it my fault that granny died?' asked an eight-year-old girl. 'I didn't carry her bag up the steps.'

Such children, who openly express their guilt, are likely to get over their disturbance quickly. It might be advisable for parents and teachers to bring guilt feelings out into the open, casually, with children who do not express their feelings. They can make sure that the child realizes that the death of a friend or relative, and particularly one who was disliked, occurred naturally and was in no way connected with the child's behaviour.

Parents, when tried to desperation by a child's behaviour, may seek the aid of a dead relative in trying to control him. 'Daddy wouldn't have liked you to do that.' Boys are still urged to be brave as their father was. But it is rare to find children today being made to take vows at death-beds and at funerals. In Victorian times it was not unusual for a girl to promise her dying father never to get married, or her dying mother that she would become 'the little mother' of ten brothers and sisters.

Anger and guilt feelings complicate matters in the young child, who may believe that his mother is *bad* for leaving him, or that he himself is somehow responsible for her death. Guilt feelings probably play a part in the grief of adults too. This is shown most effectively in the Scandinavian film *Day of Wrath*, in which a wife who wishes her husband was out of the way believes, when he drops dead with a heart attack, that she is guilty of his death and is, in fact, a witch.

Guilt may be expressed directly by an adult, 'If only I'd done more for him when he was alive,' etc, or by the child, 'Did Mummy die because I wouldn't eat my dinner and

H

worried her?' What of the child of eight, so unlike Wordsworth's little cottage girl, walking along the Embankment
chatting away to a friendly grown-up about her brother who
she said had died of typhus because he fell into the 'mucky
Thames'? When commiserated with she replied crypti-
cally: 'Serve 'im right.'

An American mortician, justifying the high cost of
funerals in the USA, said openly in a TV programme
(August 1964) that spending large sums of money on flowers,
caskets, and beautifying the dead helped to assuage guilt
feelings. One wished one had done more for the deceased
during life. It was too late now, but one could make up for
it by giving a beautiful funeral.

A woman colleague of mine who was born in the earlier
years of this century described how, as a child, she was made
to kneel on her beloved father's grave and promise never to
tell a lie. This, she said, was a major shock—'a sort of black-
ness'—from which she never recovered. This is unlikely to
happen to a bereaved child today. Nor is the modern child
expected to find the dead beautiful or 'transformed'. In *The
Threshold* (*Vor Tag*), translated from the German by D.
Rutherford, the little girl is made to look at the dressed
corpse of her little sister Irmgard through a window. Her
grandmama tells her 'the big star up there' (shining above
the dead child) is her sister's soul. Dead children were described as 'beautiful as angels', 'like little brides' in their
coffins, and the older dead had 'radiant smiles', 'heavenly
peace', and so forth. No wonder C. S. Lewis in *Surprised by
Joy* breaks out with: 'To this day I do not know what they
mean when they call dead bodies beautiful. The ugliest
man alive is an angel of beauty compared with the loveliest
of the dead.' It would be interesting to know whether
children in the USA react to the beautifying of corpses.

In the case of the bereaved child in this country today it is
difficult to tell which part of the fear and loss has done the
most damage. If such a child reveals repressed anxiety and
terrors when subjected to appropriate tests, even the most
penetrating of analysts may find it hard to determine the
relative parts played by the fear of the unknown, the actual

loss of the body, and the separation from the living, familiar person.

It is interesting to note that children's jokes about death centre on the paraphernalia of death-coffins, funerals, rather than on the actual corpses; or if these are used as subjects, they rarely are the corpses of mothers, fathers, sisters, brothers, though uncles and lovers are referred to occasionally. We get this in the well-known song *Clementine*. On the other hand, the prospect of the mother's death may be seen as a deterrent.

> Criss cross the Bible, never tell a lie,
> If I do my mother will die.

A mother reports: 'All four of my children feared death, but mainly as affecting other people, particularly me, though when John was run over he kept saying, "Am I going to die?" [aged eight]. When I said "No" he was quickly reassured. But they were very frightened of someone they love dying. They have asked: "What happens when you die?" "Why do people die?" We haven't talked about it directly. I usually say something to the effect that people usually die after they have done the work they had to do, and as to what happens, nobody really knows, but many people believe that life continues in a different way. But the main thing is dread of separation from those they love, and in their younger years this meant "us".'

One is safe enough telling children that people die when they are old and they themselves have years and years of life during a stable period of history and in a stable society. But what happens if wars and disasters overtake them? Will they accept death on a large scale more or less readily for being reassured 'while the going was good'? In Denmark a book has been published for the children of agnostics, answering their questions about death in a 'truthful' manner. But the author takes the precaution of letting these children meet their cousins who are believers, thus showing them that other points of view exist.

The trouble is that until even more work has been carried out on child development it is very difficult indeed to discover what the child is actually thinking. Children invent their own myths. This has been my own direct personal experience. A child whose questions on birth and death had been answered realistically was found to have created a myth of her own origin from the earth, where there was an 'earth lady' who looked after her and allowed her to play with the roots of plants, and death was a return there. Only when the children grow up and tell us can we be really sure, that is why autobiographical material is valuable even if there are some inaccuracies.

For instance, a small child may show fear at the sight of the dead body of a beloved relative, but there is much evidence that it is the actual removal of this body for ever which may be the basis of the traumatic experience. How far are we intensifying this experience by the rapid removal of the corpse to the mortuary or 'chapel of rest'? In cases of sudden death, are we pushing down the child's experience of bereavement into the dangerous depths of repression by hiding away the corpse so that the child never again sees the familiar body? Three examples given below reveal the complexity, perhaps the insolubility, of this problem.

In March 1963 the mother of five children, still in her thirties, died at home, after a lingering illness. The four older children reacted with 'grief and mourning' from the moment of death, but the youngest boy, aged nearly five, refused to believe that mother 'wouldn't talk again'. Only when the body was taken away for the funeral and he saw the empty bedroom did he exclaim: 'Mummy is really dead, isn't she?'

During the same month a girl of seventeen became unduly hostile to her mother's second marriage although she was fond of the new stepfather—a life-long family friend. Nothing would persuade her that her mother had a right to this new happiness. When it was pointed out that she and her two older sisters had their own boy friends and the mother was lonely she became hysterical, screaming that obviously her mother had never loved her father or she could not have tolerated a new husband. The two older sisters had been present when the father had dropped dead suddenly while

loading his motor-cycle for a fishing expedition and had reacted normally in the circumstances. But the youngest one,
aged eight, had been in bed at the time. When she awoke
next morning there was no father at all—simply that. His
body had been taken to hospital. She never saw anything
of him again and the family deliberately refrained from discussing the tragedy or even showing grief in her presence. So
she never mentioned her dead father except once. 'Now
there'll be no one to come home from work and love me and
give me some of his dinner.'

The third example has been the subject of much controversy. President Kennedy was triumphant, smiling and
happy one moment, and dead soon after. The two children,
Caroline, nearly six, John Junior, nearly three, were told of
their father's assassination the next morning. When I was
talking to a teachers' class a fortnight afterwards the subject
of death rituals cropped up and Mrs Kennedy was strongly
criticized for allowing the children to be present at so many
of the ceremonies, particularly the viewing of the catafalque.

At one time John Junior revealed his being at a very early
stage in the development of the child's thinking about death.
Given a flag to 'keep him quiet', he asked for another one 'to
give Daddy'. To him death was either reversible or it had,
as yet, no meaning. Caroline was reported to have become
withdrawn. We shall never know (unless, perhaps, in later
autobiographies and biographies) how these children reacted
at the time, or what effect the funeral rites will have on them.
Presumably, as good Catholics, they will affirm immortality,
and, as David Frost pointed out in the TW3 tribute on BBC
television, 'death is not a leveller'. Their father died in a
blaze of glory, more than life-size—near deification—and his
death would not deprive them in any material sense. But
he left them alive and he returned to them dead, and they
never saw his dead body.

Does it help to allay the sorrows of bereavement to know
that you can turn on a tape-recorder, a disc, project live
pictures, review old TV programmes, and thus still hold on to
something of 'daddy'? Will this, later on, conflict with
visions of the soul in purgatory, the soul in paradise?

Whatever the answers to these questions may be, if indeed there are any answers, bereavement involving a loved person must be experienced as a total deprivation. However marvellous are the descriptions of an after-life, nothing could possibly be better than the present one to a healthy child, and therefore, by analogy, to the unfortunate deceased. The dead are missing life—the sun, moon, sea, breakfast and dinner, shopping, presents, fun and games. 'Mummy won't be able to go blackberrying or buy a new hat' (G, aged seven). 'He'll never be able to have a bike will he?' (brother S, aged six). The dead are missing *demonstrated* love—the only sort which a child can possibly understand; and likewise the bereaved child is deprived of this love. If the dead person had been going abroad for ever, for the rest of the child's life, this, too, would have contained the one essential ingredient in bereavement—physical separation, which has been considered in the previous chapter.

A child has to be in a desperate situation before it would prefer death to life. 'If death is the gate to a better life, why do so few want to open it?' asked an adolescent when discussing capital punishment. Life sentences are preferable to practically all prisoners. The child grows up to find that adolescents and grown-ups think of death as part of the human situation which one must accept, but they will find no one courting it nowadays. The martyrs are out of fashion and the suicides are regarded as deranged. We cannot possibly tell the bereaved child that the death of any but the very old, the chronic sick, the desperate, is a 'good thing' when we all are busily avoiding it. What, then, *can* we tell the bereaved child? Very little; but perhaps one could find ceremonies which help. Perhaps it is better to face up to the sight of the dead body, experience its immobility and coldness, to realize that it is disintegrating. Perhaps the shared grief of relatives and friends and the burial or cremation rites produce a positive and overt experience of death, which in the long run is safer than a negative and covert one. Or 'the baked meats' might be revived and rejoicing over a good life safely concluded be brought into ceremonials.

Yet children themselves appear to have a horror of the

paraphernalia of death, and we are no nearer a solution if a child asks directly 'Where is my mummy now?' All we can say, in truth, is that the particles of the body will finally be distributed into earth, air, and water, part of the known universe, and may become united into living molecules again. We do not emphasize this nearly enough. Even a grief-stricken child has a strong movement towards objectivity and death in a physical sense can become an object of scientific curiosity. As for the personality, the soul, spirit, psyche, the 'inmost me', how we deal with that will be a matter for each one according to his philosophy or religion. It is essential to deal with it and at the same time to point out that other people may have different views. After this we have to deal with the life which goes on inevitably after the disappearance of the 'departed one'.

To replace the dead too soon is probably a mistake, as most parents realize. Even a pet should not immediately be replaced by a new one as this will be regarded as a sort of treason. In time new relationships will help to compensate for the old one. The child, fortunately, is growing and developing and peer group relationships, boy and girl friendships, will be strengthening and multiplying. Life, lived abundantly, will compensate in the end, but never completely. This is particularly so in the case of the death of a parent; in fact, there may be a great danger of a mother trying to take on the role of the dead father, or vice versa, and, even worse, of a child trying to play a father or mother role in order to comfort the bereaved parent. It is far better to recognize in the beginning that the dead cannot be replaced. Perhaps the only case in which it is emotionally safe to re-place the dead by the living is when a baby has died at birth or possibly in the neo-natal period. A new brother or sister may compensate the bereaved siblings and also the parents.

It has become a truism to state that the secure child will be able to deal with death more satisfactorily than an insecure one, but what still needs to be pointed out is that the more dynamic, the more creative, the more intelligent the child is, the deeper will be its feelings and the stronger its relationships. It is a fallacy to oppose intellect and feeling, creativity and objectivity. These children will suffer terribly if bereaved, but unlike the psychologically insecure child they will be able to express their sufferings in some form and objectify them.

A recent investigation by three research workers of the University of Michigan on the effect of bereavement on fifty-eight children between two and fourteen shows the effect of sibling loss to be complex and to vary with the background and maturity of the child as one would expect, but all the children had an intense fear of death and many had guilt feelings. In 25 per cent of the cases the first impact of suffering came through the parents' reactions and it was discovered that in as many as 20 per cent the parents identified the living child with the dead one, sometimes even changing the name. To nearly a third of these children growing up meant dying, and some regressed in consequence. The authors believe that the bereaved child should be treated 'at crisis point' to prevent severe and permanent personality disorders.

An interesting paper testing the hypothesis that 'Depressive illness in later years may be a reaction to a present loss or bereavement associated with loss or bereavement in childhood' was published in the *British Journal of Psychology*, Vol 107, July 1961, by Felix Brown, Psychiatrist at Hampstead General Hospital. His theory of early sensitivization seems to be borne out in the group he tested against two control groups, one from the 1921 census and the other from a general patient group in the hospital. He found that 41 per cent of the depressive group had lost a parent before the age of fifteen, compared with 12 per cent of the Census group and 10 per cent of the general patient group. Hampstead is an area with a high incidence of suicide (twice the national average). Therefore, from this preliminary survey there is some evidence that bereavement in childhood may leave a permanent sensitiveness so that a second time may result in some kind of mental illness.

Dr Brown also found himself in disagreement with Sylvia Anthony's findings that the ages eight to twelve are the most traumatic with regard to loss of parents. He found that loss of mother is significant at all ages of childhood and loss of the father is more significant in later years five to nine and ten to fourteen.

That parent loss and sibling loss may result in personality disorders is borne out by observations and reports in auto-biography, and in a covert manner in fiction, art, and poetry. There may be a sense of complete abandonment leading to aggressive acts. Erikson, in *Journal of Social Issues*, speaks of the 'shattering of the ability to trust' when a child has been deprived of a parent. This lack of trusting is a common feature in maladjusted children. The *Journal of Child Psychology and Psychiatry* published an interesting and com-prehensive article on 'Bereavement in Childhood' by Bettie Arthur and Mary Kemme as part of a project on mourning and familial loss in eighty-three emotionally disturbed child-ren. The authors begin by saying that the young child's problem is complicated by his 'intellectual inability to com-prehend the nature of death' and they find that the children they investigated, while having individual reactions, never-theless showed certain common features in their behaviour patterns.

There seems to be, at least for the few emotionally disturbed children on whom we have direct information, a characteristic reaction to the news of the death of a parent which, though varying somewhat in its individual manifestations, incorporates certain fundamental features. Immediate evasion is soon fol-lowed by superficial cognitive recognition of the fact. There is usually a transitory regression in overt behaviour while the child endeavours to absorb and integrate the emotional shock. This period is characterized by various defensive efforts to ward off, undo, and make restitution for the parent's death. There is usually a preoccupation with regaining, or finding a placement for, the lost parent, together with a conviction that personal guilt or unworthiness will preclude this eventuality. These im-mediate reactions to the information that a parent has died can be followed by more persistent change in the child's personality when he is unsuccessful in attempting to integrate the trauma.

In her book *Fatherless Families*, published in 1964, Mar-garet Wynn estimates that 7 per cent of all dependent child-dren in the United Kingdom are fatherless and of these 33 per cent have been deprived of the male parent by death, and her survey reveals the inadequacy of the financial support given to widows with young children and the problems that arise in such families owing to poverty, apart from other deprivations.

'The literature of the world on fatherless families is extensive,' she says, and goes on to point out that 'there has never been a review of the effect of paternal deprivation on mental health which can in any way be compared with that of Dr Bowlby and his colleagues on maternal deprivation'. While evidence is increasing that father deprivation may cause personality disturbances in a society based on the nuclear family it is certainly true that maternal loss in the early years is a much more profound deprivation, being based on biological need. Recent work on monkeys deprived of mothers and even given foster mothers suggests that this sort of loss is devastating in primates.

There is another type of bereavement which so far, fortunately, has not been the lot of children in this country. This is loss of the social group as well as that of individual relatives and friends. Jewish children experienced this as recently as the thirties and forties of this century both in Germany and elsewhere where pogroms occurred. In Lidice all males of the village over the age of fourteen were shot, and the younger children were sent away from their community. Records are only just coming through which may give some idea of how these deprived children faced the future.

Martha Wolfenstein describes the 'disaster syndrome' in terms of lack of emotion, and docility, *at the time*:

A witness at Hiroshima described 'The silence in the grove by the river where hundreds of gruesomely wounded suffered together. . . . the hurt ones were quiet; no one wept, much less screamed in pain, no one complained, none of the many who died did so noisily, not even the children cried, very few people even spoke.'

Speaking of a hurricane disaster, she says:

Also the fact of death had intruded itself abruptly into the children's sphere. Most of the children of the town knew some child who was killed. But death is a subject which parents generally have difficulty in discussing with their children, and about which they are apt not to be very candid. So, for instance, if a child asks whether he could die, that one dies when one gets very old. Such reasons are disproved.

But the greatest emotional distress was associated with abandonment. Survivors of disasters, though they might feel self-reproach for being alive while others died, mingled of course with its opposite, self-congratulation, soon recovered, but those who survived alone took longer to recover. A child standing alone in agony of terror and distress is well portrayed in the Italian film of the Second World War, *Paise!* All have been killed in his farm in a battle between Germans, English, and partisans and he is alone, utterly desolate. Bereavement in these circumstances is obviously a most devastating experience. Many children in Europe were actually present when their parents were shot or dragged off to concentration camps. Even in England, which has escaped invasion and major revolution, children witnessed the death of relatives in air raids and experienced abandonment.

Bereavement in adolescence and adulthood may change a negative attitude to one's own death to a positive one. Where the dead has been deeply loved there may be a desire on the part of the bereaved to die too, in order not to be separated. This is most vividly shown in the case of lovers and is the tragedy of Romeo and Juliet. There may also be a desire to have died instead of the beloved one—'If only I could have died in his place.'

A poem, written by a child on the verge of adolescence in the nineteen-sixties, uses strangely old-fashioned imagery—which children do, in fact, often use—but also reveals a personal and deeply felt 'knowledge' of bereavement.

TIME AND DEATH

(eleven-year-old girl)

My parents each saw a man and a woman
Whom I see today.
They are time and death, time and death
Who took my parents away.

The man was old, so very old
His hair was long and grey.
He carried a sickle on his back, on his back,
And he took my parents away.

The woman was thin, so very thin
She had around her a glow.
She had two wings on her back, on her back,
As I well now know.

They've taken kings, they've taken queens,
They've taken memory too
In bygone days and recent ones
And now I'm going too.

Twelve

KILLING

Killing, the final act of aggression, appears to be an aspect of death more easily understood by the child than any other. Indeed, he very frequently uses the word 'kill' in his definition of death. 'When Jesus kills you in the night' was the reply given by a four-year-old when the question of what 'die' meant came up in casual conversation. In the beginning of his autobiography Bernard Darwin quotes the 'young gentleman of five' who says with some satisfaction 'I'll bet you're killed before me' and then, as an afterthought, added 'and my mummy too'. The same child begged his mother not to die before he was old enough to go to the cinema by himself.

It would appear from these and similiar instances that the very young child does not distinguish very readily between being killed and dying naturally. Some animated force—a person, an animal, or a god—is the causal agent in death. In this respect he is very close to primitive peoples who also may believe that death is due to some animated principle outside one's control, probably a supernatural one. But as the child, in trying to understand his own aggressive impulses, will sometimes identify himself with the 'killer' when a loved one dies, guilt feelings, which as we have seen are associated with bereavement, may become excessive.

Sylvia Anthony, writing over twenty years ago, stresses the important part played by animals in helping the child to overcome what she refers to as the death wish—a psychological concept which is somewhat out of fashion today and may imply an unconscious desire to get rid of someone. 'Thus live things which can be killed with impunity are animals, and if you have wished someone dead, and it was a human being, you are guilty, but if it was an animal you are

innocent and safe. Those against whom we have death wishes
which we cannot admit without shame and guilt are represented in our fantasies as animals.'

As late as 1964 in this country there was killing by execution for capital murder. Both children and adolescents show
concern about this, often revealing what a greatly disturbing
effect an execution has on them. Teachers in schools near a
prison where an execution has taken place report particularly difficult behaviour among the children. Executions
appear in children's art, writing, and drama, but rarely are
they directly associated with a recent event. A ten-year-old
'A' stream in a Junior school (1962) all contributed to a class
magazine. They were given a free hand to write on anything
they liked, including a news and current affairs section. One
boy asked if they could write about any murders. I said they
could. The idea was acclaimed with general glee and there
were several whispered references to the 'A6'. In actual
fact, they managed to cover most of the week's news from
Colonel Glenn to the Grand National, but no child wrote a
word about the A6 or any other murder.

What about other types of killing—those which may have
grown-up approval? Most of these appear in history and
fiction. There are the glamorous rebels defying what they
believe to be the forces of evil—the 'goodys' against the
'badys', but it is very difficult for the child to tell whether a
given killing is supposed to be laudable or blameworthy.
A boy of seven taken to see *Julius Caesar* watched spell-
bound, but remarked finally, 'Is Brutus meant to be a goody
or a bady?'—a question very hard to answer. What of Davy
Crocket, Robin Hood, William Tell, King Arthur—all of
which have been glamorized on TV?

Individuals 'killing in a good cause' in legend and history
seem to have the approval of grown-ups, and it is only after
puberty that children really start to question this good cause.
Dying at the hands of society because of one's beliefs is also
accepted as good and brave because on the whole that is
what we still teach. Jesus, Socrates, Joan of Arc, and all the
'noble army of martyrs' were acceptable to the older generation until one really started to think of Galileo. I have heard

several school-teachers recently fall down on that famous re-
cantation, and very few had the sense to point out that he
wrote one of his most important works *after* his apparent
humiliation.

In my childhood we used to chant

> Cowardy, cowardy custard
> Ate a pound of mustard

after any boy who refused to fight in a just cause, but we
were equally capable of singing:

> He who fights and runs away
> Will live to fight another day,
> But he who is in battle slain
> Will never live to fight again.

Martyrdom is less acceptable to modern children and their
attitude to it does not have to be covered up by rhymes and
jokes.

In other cultures, and at other times (notably in Japan),
death by suicide has had the approval of society. To fall on
one's sword, to open a vein rather than live on in disgrace or
bring disgrace to family and country, was regarded as right.
The protest burnings of Buddhists recently was commented
on by a junior schoolboy of nine as 'Phoney'.

Durkheim, in his book *Le Suicide*, states that suicide is extremely rare among children, and the earliest recorded age
which was 'wholly exceptional' was five. It occurs more in
civilized than in uncivilized communities, more in cities than
in the country. It is commoner in males, in the divorced,
in the USA among Whites than Negroes. Of course, actual
suicide in Britain today is regarded by most as the result of
illness and children are told that—if anyone in the family
commits suicide. One such case came to my notice a few
years ago in an infant school. A little boy, aged six, from
time to time lay on the classroom floor and screamed, so that
the student in charge was unable to cope. He had gone home
one day and found his mother dead from self-administered
gas.

Suicide of a grown-up is more terrifying to a child than

murder, and those who have encountered it react with something even more disturbing than terror. Emlyn Williams
describes the discovery of a hanged man in a slaughterhouse
in one of the villages in which he grew up:

It was as if there had been a deafening explosion, every window shattered, and now me alone in a silent room with a sleeping baby and a dog. My knees were locked to my stool; I felt
my face white. . . . For all was changed. Ismael Jones, a farmer
with a beard whom I had beheld in the distance, a human being
like any other who had been a baby like the one asleep at my
feet. . . . A pair of boots, gently swinging.

He stays awake imagining himself trying to stop the man from
killing himself but cannot:

He is lighting a stub of candle; the naked corpses of swine
hang motionless, their great shadows swinging over us. He is
Dad, Dad with a beard; he is fastening the noose, with the
method of the drunken and the damned, and for the first time in
the history of the world a child looks up into the face of a man
about to . . . I made myself count sheep.'

The child 'George', of course, always 'used' such events for
his imaginary book 'George, his Story'. He goes on to describe the bathos introduced by a grown-up: 'Questioning
John, I was envious enough to be relieved when all he had to
contribute was: "I ran in and I thought it was an extra pig,
then I saw it had got trousers on and I ran out." '

Suicide, then, in our country today is never applauded but
rarely condemned. The factors leading to suicide are still a
matter of debate, many psychologists inclining towards
Freud's theories of the 'psychodynamics of suicide' while
many sociologists still support Durkheim, who stated in
Le Suicide (1897) that 'a major factor in suicide is the loss of
sympathetic acceptance of an individual by his social group'.
In an interesting paper published in The Scientific American in
1954 Don Jackson sums up his own position in a 'general
picture' which combines the psychological and the sociological approaches:

An individual, generally in a sociological setting that comple-
ments his interpersonal difficulties, attempts suicide unless he
experiences specific rejection (real or illusory) in a situation which
mimics an earlier traumatic one. The essence of the interpersonal

difficulties is a strong feeling of loss of love, with consequent hateful and murderous feelings. The specific rejection is experienced at a time when a person's psychic economy is already strained to the utmost by the notion that he is unacceptable, and by strong guilt feelings. In seeking death he seeks expiation and reincarnation . . .

Jackson mentions that 'children seldom commit suicide but when they do they illustrate the underlying motives more clearly than adults'—e.g. an adolescent girl who feared she might kill her mother in the night (not taken seriously) attempted suicide. A ten-year-old boy hanged himself when his father was killed in the War.

It seems untrue to say that the 'roots of suicide always lie in childhood conflicts'. The Buddhists who recently burned themselves alive as a political protest, those who are prepared 'to fast unto death', surely act according to abstract ideas rather than to solve personal problems, rooted in infancy.

It is probably true that suicides have strong fears of death and suffer from 'sorrowful separation' before the act, in fantasy. Most who remember their adolescent fantasies will be able to recall dreams of suicide especially in the earlier years, most of them including heart-broken relatives whom they wish to punish. Karl Menninger believes suicide to be 'a paradox' in that the 'one who wished to kill himself does not wish to die' and several investigators such as Jensen and Petty (*Psychoanalytical Quarterly*, 1958) find the 'fantasy of rescue' very marked in attempted suicide. A recent Pelican publication on suicide by Stengel states that only 'one in six or eight' of suicidal acts have a fatal outcome and there are about 100 acts annually per 100,000 of the population of Britain.

Are there other types of killing which have the approval of society in Britain today? There is the killing of animals, plants, and micro-organisms. Children readily accept the killing of germs and of plants as these are regarded as non-sentient, though some do have qualms. Germs, regarded as doers of evil, sometimes actually arouse the aggressive urges of children, who have been seen to stab drawings of spirochaetes with pencils. I remember a project on germs with top

I

juniors carried out by a student, and following a rather too forceful description the class divided into germs and white blood corpuscles in the playground and fought . . . Even in GCE 'O' Level biology candidates answering a question on the functions of the blood often say 'the white corpuscles *fight* disease organisms'. Animals, and by animals children often mean mammals, and to an advanced age tend to exclude insects, are a very different matter. Society sanctions the killing of animals for food, in self-defence, in order to save crops, etc, for scientific experiment, and also certain kinds of animals may be killed for sport. What is the child to make of all this? Sooner or later most children question the use of animals for food. Most accept it eventually as part of the 'nature of things' though some become vegetarian later on. Again most accept the killing of insects by sprays, but when the story-book animal, the rabbit, was killed by myxomatosis many were deeply disturbed. In the depths of childhood this was 'Benjamin Bunny', 'Peter Rabbit', and, later the live pet in the hutch. Children who keep white mice appear to regard them as in a different category from the house mouse and may accept the trapping of the one, or killing by the cat, and weep tears over the death of the other kind. Mice, however, are animals which still come into story-books, and attitudes to their deaths are found to be confused.

Children who come to accept as natural the killing of animals for food may be troubled about the killing of animals for scientific purposes and later on are apt to query the ethics of vivisection. I was in a London Junior School when there was an outcry in the Press about unwanted kittens and cats which it was alleged a school had asked the children to bring for dissection. It was a time when the price of rabbits was prohibitive and rats had not come into general use. Rats from a scientific dealer cost 7s 6d each in any case. The children *without exception* in a top junior class were horrified about cats being used for such a purpose though some of them would have accepted mice, rats, and even rabbits.

The anti-vivisection society takes upon itself to parade the streets with displays and posters from time to time and children may approach the class teacher for 'opinions' about the ethics of using live animals for scientific investigations. In several cases children have been satisfied when told that the animal is painlessly killed if it cannot recover or if further living would be unpleasant. There was, however, a great deal of criticism by teachers of a film-strip on Food aimed at the top juniors and lower forms of secondary schools because it showed a child carrying out experiments on vitamin deficiencies, using rabbits. The reactions of a junior class to a dissection has been described in a previous chapter.

The first stirrings of rebellion against 'God' often arise when the child first becomes aware of the carnage in the animal kingdom. Children as young as six or seven have verbalized their confusions. They may have been taught that there is an all-powerful, benevolent Creator. 'Why does God let the cat kill the baby bird?' 'I cannot believe in a Creator. If I did I would have to admit that he is an exceedingly cruel one,' Bertrand Russell said. The child is often in the same position.

What are children to make of the killing of animals for sport? Cock-fighting is no longer sanctioned by society, though from time to time it is said to take place in remote areas. Fox-hunting is justified by those who do it on the grounds that fox are vermin, but sportsmen cannot find such a convenient argument for deer-hunting and the bagging of birds. Among the sophisticated there seems to be a recent tendency to take their children to see bullfights while in Spain on holiday. I asked one such parent whether she thought this a sensible thing to do. She justified it on artistic grounds, saying the colour and movement was so glorious. If children's parents sanction 'Death in the afternoon' in one way or another (for men and bulls may die), what effect is this likely to have on children's attitudes to the killing of animals (or men) for sport?

Having examined society's attitudes to killing, what can be discovered about the children's attitudes in relation to that society? Is there, in man, an innate desire to kill? It is impossible here to discuss various theories of aggression. Biologically, aggression in animals is certainly associated

with at least three major processes—viz. sexual rivalry, feeding, and claiming and defence of territory. Feeding may be
regarded as an aggressive act *in itself* and is certainly prim-
ordial. Amoeba 'swallowing' by ingesting a food particle is
aggressive in this sense and those psychologists who regard
the baby at the breast as one in a state of 'naked aggression'
may be biologically correct, though to say that the baby
'believes' he is destroying the breasts by feeding seems somewhat exaggerated (Winnicott). In the higher animals
sexual activity is so complicated that it is difficult to general-
ize, but that aggression plays a part is beyond doubt.
Whether in the sex act itself the male is wholly aggressive is
open to question. What is particularly interesting here is the
suggestion that the impulse to kill is closely associated with
the sex urge in the male. As in human societies, by and large,
the males are the killers, it is an hypothesis which deserves
close examination. Reich, author of the *Sexual Revolution*,
believes, as do many anarchists, that a complete liberation of
sexual urges from moral codes would remove the frustration
which arouses the urge to destroy and kill. There is something in this, although in those primitive societies in which
sexual behaviour is permissive killing still goes on, and there
is a tendency among modern anthropologists to regard the
socialization of the sex urges with corresponding restraints as
a step forward in the evolution of human societies as distinct
from primate 'hordes'.

One might note here two relevant characteristics of the
contemporary teenagers. Sexually many of them behave
permissively and a large proportion of these are anti-bomb.
On the other hand, delinquent males in this age group are
both aggressive sometimes to the point of murder *and* sexually
permissive.

Whatever theories one may hold about aggression, in
civilized communities, and indeed to some degree in all
human societies, certain manifestations of it have been regarded as permissible and even good, while others have been
regarded as anti-social In fact, there is a tendency among
male parents and teachers to welcome manifestations of the
'fighting spirit' in small boys as signs of manhood.

During the Second World War, when killing for one's country was regarded as necessary, when as Winnicott says the country *counts on* adolescent aggression, what happened to the children? There were many detailed observations made on evacuated children, on children during raids; standardized tests were used, reports issued, but to my mind none of these are as convincing as two novels written about a group of children during war. One is Joyce Cary's *Charlie is My Darling* and the other *Lord of the Flies* by William Golding.

The problem of violence, particularly of acts of aggression within a community in peace-time in the form of gang warfare between adolescents and young men, with occasional killings, is one which so far our society has failed to solve. Various factors have been held to be responsible, among them TV and films, horror comics and other sadistic literature, lack of adventure in towns, segregation of children at eleven-plus, but as Professor H. J. Eysenck suggests in a most penetrating article in *The New Scientist* (No 264, December 7, 1961), 'There should be a careful laboratory investigation of well-documented research' before we draw conclusions regarding the increase in crimes of violence.

Killing, basically, belongs to the male of the human species. From the nursery onwards one hears boys threatening to kill far more than we hear girls. Boys, too, discuss the meaning and the effects of killing more openly than girls. An interesting example of varying aspects of killing games observed in the space of a quarter of an hour in a nursery class of four-year-olds is given below. The girls were painting, playing house and shop, or quietly examining books.

The boys had made a model which they called 'Battle of India' on a large sand-tray. They kept adding to it. There was a painted sea, trees made of twigs, forts, ships, figures, etc. Although they had labelled it 'Battle of India' the three boys who were playing with the model said that the ships were German and English and the English were killing most of the Germans. Within a few minutes both sides were completely wiped out.

Two boys playing outside the classroom, at the same time, lay down rather carefully. One sat up and said, 'I'm dead.

He's killed me', and flopped down again. The other then half-sat up too and said: 'I'm dead. He's killed me.' The first shouted: 'I'm really dead. I can't open my eyes so I am dead.' 'So am I. I can't open my eyes.'

A little farther away in the nursery garden two boys were discussing a worm they had found. One said: 'Worms don't die because they are soft. You can knock their mouths off but they don't die. You can't kill worms. Human beings die because they are hard.' (He hit his own chest.)

On the same afternoon, in another school, three boys were crayoning in the classroom while the rest were in the Hall.

JAMES: 'I dreamt Stephen got locked up in prison and I knocked the policeman down and rescued him.'

STEPHEN: 'I'm the best at drawing in this class.'

MARK: 'I dreamt James was killing me and I flew away at eighty miles an hour.'

STEPHEN: 'An arrow killed you.'

JAMES: 'It's smashing to be killed. I'd like to shoot everyone in the world and I'd kill all the mothers dead.'

MARK: 'Yes, we'd kill everyone's mothers except our own.'

HENRY comes in: 'We'd kill them all' (*jumping into the air and pretending to shoot*).

I asked: 'What would you do with all the people when you had killed them?'

'Bury them.'

'But would there be room?'

HENRY: 'We'd eat them all up and gnaw their bones.'

MARK: 'And their blood.'

HENRY: 'The lions could eat some.'

All except Stephen then leapt around pretending to kill until their attention was diverted.

Marian (aged three years five months, adopted at two) shows an unusual amount of aggression in which threats to kill feature frequently, but death is synonymous with all forms of destruction. She threatens loudly to kill Auntie, to put her all squashed up in a dustbin, to throw her on the bonfire and burn her all up, to chop her head right off. She punishes her dolls violently though so far has not killed them.

Controversy is still going on as to whether children who

appear to be excessively interested in killing and play violent
games almost exclusively are potential delinquents or merely
acting out aggression in a healthy way; obviously it depends
on a multiplicity of associated factors. Nor is it at all clear
whether one of the factors contributing to increase in crimes
of violence may be the showing of television and film programmes, though there have been cases in which juvenile
delinquents have stated that a TV programme put the idea
of violence into their heads. Sometimes actual techniques
of violence have been imitated.

It is not the place of this book to discuss the pleasure element in killing except to remind ourselves that even the
most pacificist have experienced this at some time and
particularly in childhood, if only in fantasy.

Some reactions of children tested to find out how violence
may appear in their fantasies are quoted below.

Examples of violent responses to pictures—TAT test.
(Picture of steps leading to a closed door, very brightly
coloured, no suggestion of gloom.)

Michael (aged ten, from school in very poor area): 'Behind the door there is a black car with a dead body in tied
up with string and gagged; there are water and old deck-
chairs standing against the wall and old junk. Blood all
over the floor, another man hanging from the roof-top dead
as a stone, skeletons hanging from the ceiling, coffin lying
on the floor.'

Out of thirty children in this class of ten-year-olds five
brought in violence in some form.

A matching group in a school in an area with most parents
in occupational grades 1 and 2 (Registrar General's social
grading). No one mentioned anything to do with death or
violence in reference to this particular picture, though a more
definitely suggestive picture did occasionally call forth this
sort of response. The sort of things they expected to find
behind the door were garden tools, a family picnic, the road
to the sea. This group was asked to imagine going up the
steps in the dark. Again there was no mention of personal
violence, though seventeen referred to accidents and four
referred to fear of what might be there.

It is interesting to note that while small children play games of shooting and enjoy pretending to kill and to die ('I love all and I love the killings' declared a six-year-old boy when asked about his preference on TV) only 6 per cent of 361 children aged eight to ten-plus mentioned violence in sentence completion tests which started 'the brothers were quarrelling'. Yet their paintings were often warlike and spattered with red paint. It may be that children think adults are against violent expression in the written word and their compositions are expected to be decorous.

Violence in children's paintings is an interesting field for research quite apart from psychological interpretation of individual pictures. In one infant school class observed over a year it was found that violent pictures seemed to occur in 'epidemics' and often started from non-violent subjects. For example, ships, which most small boys love to paint, started off without guns in the first paintings done by children, later ones acquired guns, and finally the pictures were full of blood, shipwrecks, drownings. The class scrap-books were filled with these, most children having 'caught' the violent representations. Aeroplanes started in a similar manner, though the crashes usually came early on. Houses, typically painted by girls but also by groups of boys, were non-violent until a fire brigade appeared in the area, then pictures became full of burnings.

In schools where children are asked to illustrate Bible and other stories, wild animals, soldiers, and monsters are dragged in, in some cases to relieve the boredom of such a task. War pictures are not necessarily prevalent when a war is actually on (see Chapter Fourteen). With normal children violence is often an excuse to use vivid colours, especially in schools where their use is restricted and you have to justify a demand for more red. Execution scenes may be painted to illustrate history in junior schools, but they are so often thought to be unjustified by teachers except with reference to the Crucifixion that they are not often found in 'creative painting'. Yet children do portray hangings, etc, in doodles and in out-of-school drawings. In adolescence such drawings may become complicated by symbols, as one of a thirteen-year-old which showed a tree wreathed with snakes and a man hanging from it. Both the tree and the man had arrows through their 'hearts'.

Children's books today rarely have violent illustrations, in marked contrast to earlier ones such as *Pilgrim's Progress* and *Grimm's Fairy Tales*. Instead, children see more up-to-date and realistic kinds of killings on television and these do appear in some of their art.

Parents are often puzzled about what attitude to take with children who seem to be preoccupied with violence in their games and creative activities. Should this killing be played out in the relative safety of childhood, where it can also be controlled and diverted, or should it be discouraged from the very beginning? Other questions may include: 'Why do boys show a greater tendency to violence than girls?' These questions can only be answered in relation to adult society. It would appear that both teachers and parents should rethink their ideas about boys, as males are the main killers in our society. Even in the nursery they are often encouraged to play more violently than girls, and the notion of 'sissy' or 'chicken' dies hard. Permissive, non-violent societies, provided there is a secure family and social framework, have been more peaceful than authoritarian ones which have regarded the manly virtues as aggressive ones. However, the problem is extremely complicated and is referred to here only in passing. Presumably most teachers and parents would prefer their children to grow up with an abhorrence of violence and to regard death by violent means as anti-social.

Thirteen

THE ADOLESCENT AND DEATH

The human being, sooner or later, will suddenly stand stock-still, gasping for breath, seeing the world for the first time, face to face. Sometimes this happens quite literally, and it may be repeated at times throughout life as is so well described in the Greek novel *Zorba*. He may be walking, playing, driving, cycling, working, reading, when he stops frozen in his tracks. What on earth is it all for? Why am I here? What are all those different shapes and colours doing? How did it start, and for heaven's sake why? How *odd* everything is! Why all those summer flowers and croaking frogs? Whoever, whatever, thought them up? And what's the good of Me? Me who will die too.

It is the utter *strangeness* of the universe which strikes dumb the human creature as he is precipitated from childhood into this second birth. Often this change takes place in our society during the years we call adolescence, but not necessarily so. It has been reported in infancy, childhood, and maturity, though it appears more often in the period of puberty and may be accompanied by ecstasy. In her book *Ecstasy* Marghanita Laski states that the popular idea that children experience ecstasy is erroneous. That may be because of a confusion between two terms—'wonder' and 'ecstasy'. Children certainly experience wonder, the kind which includes curiosity. 'The first wonder,' says Coleridge, 'is born of innocence. The second of experience.' Even these terms, used with such vital and specific meaning by the Romantic Poets (and here we might include Blake) have a very different connotation for us. We are not even sure, as post-Freudians, whether innocence has any meaning at all. But whatever we call it the first sentient experience of the universe which is linked to awareness differs in *kind* from any

others, and how the person concerned deals with it will
determine, in a large measure, the direction of his 'spiritual'
life. It has been expressed in symbolic terms as drinking of
the living water, and he who drinks it shall never thirst
again.

Autobiographies in prose and verse abound in references to
this first awareness and its determining influence:

> Sudden, thy shadow fell on me;
> I shrieked, and clasped my hands in ecstasy!
> I vowed that I would dedicate my powers
> To thee and thine—have I not kept the vow?
> (Shelley, *Hymn to Intellectual Beauty*)

But those who write of this experience have been literate men
and women, mostly exceptional people distinguished by
talent or genius. Do most 'ordinary' humans experience
something of this sudden awareness of the 'Mysterious
Universe'. There is a good deal of evidence that they do.
We cannot tell what the initiated adolescents of a primitive
tribe may feel during the rituals. We merely interpret their
ecstatic movements in the dance and incantations in terms of
our own language. We are on safer ground examining the
adolescents in our own society. Since we have become interested in child development and have devised means of
assessing it, what used to be the 'private world of childhood'
has become open to inspection. Some of the techniques used
in personality tests may seem to 'miss the whole child' in
being, of necessity, analytical. Those which are not only
empirical but also so closely in line with the physical sciences
in that they make use of physiological reactions such as pulse
rate, sweat excretion, hormone secretion, brain rhythms,
etc, also may seem out of place when used in trying to determine the strength of emotional reactions to given situations.
If someone devised a test for ecstasy, what would it reveal
except that that state occurred and in such and such a
strength? Nevertheless, such empirical tests are useful in a
given context and have shown already common factors in
human emotional development.

Teenagers have thrown light on their own development,
individually and in groups, by speaking and discussing, and

although one must discount some of their reporting as being exhibitionist and confused there is evidence from tape-recordings of youth clubs, school debates, conversations with leaders, teachers, clergy, parents, and each other, that many adolescents are 'awe-inspired' when they first become aware of life and death; and this is not confined to the talented, to the poet and artist. Even the slow learner in the special school and the disturbed and maladjusted may go through some sort of transformation. Henceforth, his attitudes to death take on a different colour. They are tinged with a new kind of loneliness:

> I, a stranger, and afraid
> In a world I never made.

In our society little attempt is made to help the adolescent in his rebirth, still less to recognize that he is involved in a sort of death. Just as we evade the problems aroused by fear of physical death in childhood, rarely referring to it unless the child directly asks, and even then giving unsatisfactory, quick answers, so we leave the adolescent to mourn in solitude over the death of his childhood, condemn the rituals of the gangs he forms in place of the groups of initiates we fail to help him to form, despise the dress and ornaments he puts on to help him to put away childish things, and look on with terror while he establishes new mores because we will not let him adopt the sexual and social codes, the habits of the adult world. But we have fed him so well during childhood, we have given him fresh air, exercise, light and adaptable clothing, we have brought him up far more permissively than we ourselves were brought up, that when he stands on the threshold of adolescence he is a very big, strong child who, if he chooses, can do what he likes.

Parents today are said to be frightened of their adolescent children. So are many teachers, particularly in schools containing children who feel 'second-rate adolescents' because they believe (and often correctly) that the first-rate ones highly approved of by society (parents and teachers) are those who passed the eleven-plus. A cap, blazer, tunic or grey flannels, polished, sensible shoes, GCE, distinguish one set of teenagers from the other, who may be forced by head-masters to imitate the first set for five days of the week but for the rest tear around in jeans and new style hair-cuts if they are boys, and tight skirts, stiletto heels, and heavy make-up if they are girls. In *Problems of Adolescent Girls* James Hemming says 'Society gets the adolescents it deserves.' Disgusted by the rival gangs in *West Side Story*, the barman says to one of the hooligans, 'You make the world lousy.' 'That's the way we found it,' is the youth's quick reply.

According to some anthropologists, including Margaret Mead and Ruth Benedict, adolescence need not be a period of turmoil. *Coming of Age in Samoa* and *Growing up in New Guinea* have a widespread popularity in the country and many modern parents realize that whereas in Samoa a child could pass smoothly from adolescence to adulthood, in New Guinea the change was sudden and drastic. Some primitive cultures were permissive with children but rigorous at puberty. Others scarcely recognized any period in between childhood and adulthood. Whatever we may learn from the examination of primitive societies and from psychological studies of adolescence, whether we subscribe to Freud's, Jung's, Adler's, or some other psychologist's interpretation of adolescent behaviour, we cannot escape from the basic physiological facts of growth and development. The human child may not undergo such a striking metamorphosis as a frog or a butterfly, nevertheless he does suffer a change. The form of child has gone never to return. The 'body image' is different. No longer is the outline of the boy very like that of the girl. Whatever culture the child belongs to there is some kind of rebirth, some kind of death, some kind of new awareness as the adult emerges.

Whether or not we subscribe to the various theories of infant sexuality, there is a great deal of difference between having no actual capacity for sexual relationship and re-production and being capable of enjoying intercourse and producing a child. The little boy may have his Oedipus and the little girl her Electra manifestations, but they are very different from the actual act of incest or even of being able potentially to perform that act. Similarly, the virgin child may feel sexual desires, but there is a vast difference between this and the actual loss of virginity.

Although it is now over sixty years ago since G. Stanley Hall wrote *Adolescence: its Psychology and its Relations to Physiology, Anthropology, Sociology, Sex, Crime, and Education*, there is much in it that is relevant to the study of adolescence today. Hall, to many modern observers, over-emphasized the theory of new birth at adolescence, but although further investigations in the anthropological, biological, and sociological fields have thrown much more light on development during these years no one can deny that there is some kind of irreversible change—one of the characteristics of birth and of death.

In this time of rapid scientific advancement and shifting social and ethical values one new set of teenage mores follows another in succession. Moreover, it is very difficult to disentangle the multitude of stimuli bombarding the adolescent from all sides. One cannot isolate a variable such as sociological background because immediately a hundred more variables raise their heads, such as ownership of television sets, the knowledge of economic spending, intelligence rating, and so on. Also, on every side, teenagers are being wooed. The big businessmen woo them by advertisement— they are a most important consumer group. The Churches try to woo them for religion. The Government woos them for technology. When Sylvia Anthony used her modified Geneva Story Completion test in her investigation of the child's attitudes to death in 1939, Story 10 ran as follows: 'Then the fairy said: "You are growing into a big boy: do you want to be big and grown-up, or would you like to stay a child for a long time, perhaps for always?"' When I first used this story in 1961 I found it needed considerable modification. Not only was it usually necessary to omit the fairy but the children quickly informed me that there were not just children and grown-ups but teenagers also, and many of them would like to be teenagers.

Although there has been a great deal of literature on adolescence in Western and other societies since Hall wrote, it is still an unmapped territory compared with that of the primary school child. This is partly because teachers in our secondary schools have been more concerned with the learning of subjects than in the development of the child, and at best have had only one year of teacher training, much of this being occupied in methodology. What young teachers in grammar schools in particular know of adolescent development has come largely from their own recollection of it as a period through which they themselves have just passed.

The adolescent attitudes to death in English society today is an enormous field of work waiting to be explored. Here I can only touch on it, with some examples from discussion groups and from individual teenagers.

Gesell's *Youth*, which regards adolescence as a cycle of growth from eleven into the twenties, shows it to be a 'consistent ripening process' during the crucial years from ten to sixteen, which includes puberty, but already, in reading through his norms of development in the American children he studied, we find that not only American adolescents but ours, too, do not necessarily correspond to those of even a few years ago. I shall refer now only to attitudes to death.

In view of the recent report on 'Teenage Religion', it is interesting to note that Gesell finds that ideas about reincarnation are expressed by a few eleven-year-olds, but these occur most frequently at age twelve; ideas about heaven as a reward for good behaviour occur even among sixteen-year-olds (but surely not much now?). As these findings are based on direct questions to normal adolescents, together with observations from parents, staff, and a team of investigators by the personal interview method, naturally the study is only partial. Other investigators using projective tests, art, poetry, etc, have helped to delve more deeply into motivation of adolescent behaviour.

Is there any aspect of an adolescent's attitude to death which he does not share with those of his age group in previous generations or in other cultures? As far as I have investigated there is, and it is connected with mass death as distinct from individual death. I remember at a gathering of young people met together to look at pictures of Hiroshima a speaker said that one could only think of death in terms of *one* death, the death of a given individual. But such an idea is greeted with horror by adolescents—*of course*, they say, it is worse to kill a million people than five hundred. What about the extermination of six million Jews—not only is the death of six million individuals worse in terms of individual suffering but, more than that, something bigger, something cultural, is destroyed.

When the USA started to make fall-out shelters instead of swimming-pools and fitted them up with gadgets, putting across the view that some would survive a nuclear war, adolescent fury mounted high. This, however, was not inconsistent with their belief that the *quantity* of people killed matters; they simply did not believe that there could be any survivors and regarded the propaganda as false. Shakespeare realized that several deaths can be worse than one. When Macduff is told that Macbeth has had his wife and children murdered he cries: 'What *all* my pretty ones? Did you say *all*?' And Bertrand Russell has said that a tragedy which one could scarcely recover from wholly would be if *all* one's children died.

The death of the human species to many thinking adolescents is not only a tragedy but an affront. It is an affront to all those primitive ancestors who dared to become men, emerging from the primates, taking ever greater risks. We have to remember that the adolescent today, even more so than the child, is steeped in evolutionary knowledge. He neither believes in the Fall of Man nor God's purpose for the human race as such. If he believes in God, it is in someone who may have universes 'teeming with life' to his credit, or, on the other hand, in a spiritual force which may not be concerned with material creation and destruction.

The adolescent, at times, like the child, is worried about his own death, the death of relatives—of 'sorrowful separation'—but he also becomes concerned about its meaning and therefore, too, about the meaning of birth, of human life. It is bad enough, to him, if the human individual is to disappear for ever. How much worse if the entire species is to vanish without a trace and the whole of human history to be negated! In cultures where the individual is merged in the community (USSR, China) death in this sense is wholly tragic.

The second aspect which appears to be new to this generation of adolescents is the already changing nature of birth and sex and reproduction which have always been inextricably bound up with death in the adolescent unconscious. Sexual intercourse and reproduction have been divorced from each other by widely adopted birth control techniques. The far-seeing adolescent can already understand reproduction without sexual intercourse. Already artificial insemination occurs in humans as well as in animals. Likewise he can view birth and even gestation unconnected with a mother's body. A cartoon has already appeared in a sixth form, cut out from a leading daily. Two children are talking, and one says to the other: 'You don't *still* believe in that fairy story about the mummy's tummy, do you?' Facts of life change and with them facts of death. As has been pointed out earlier, what appears to worry the older adolescents in sixth forms I have investigated is what used to be called 'tinkering with human nature'. The cracking of the genetic code with possibilities of altering heredity, injections, brain-washing, the creation of life in petri dishes, the indefinite prolongation of life by use of artificial organs— all these things make the adolescent ask: 'Would a creature altered like this, brought into being like this, made "immortal" in this way, be recognizable as a human being? Wouldn't it be some kind of superman—a different species no more on our level than we are on a monkey's level?'

The more profound among them query the desirability of extending the life-span indefinitely and in doing so come back again to the age-old question, 'Is death functional?' Many find that it is, pointing out as philosophers still do that without an ending there would be no beginning, and without an ending all human motivation might cease—if one had all eternity to perform in, would one do anything at all, let alone create works of art? Others, however, believe that life might then be timeless as in childhood and creative activity would be unspoiled by utilitarianism. We would create and strive solely for the joy of it and all things would become pure.

K

Meanwhile there is the 'here and now'. If modern adolescents are conscious that their expectation of life may be only a few years, so were many of their predecessors in the First World War. 'We knew when we were eighteen we would be called up,' writes a public schoolboy in 1915, 'and we watched the school honours list of those killed in action grow longer each month. Most of us didn't expect to grow up, but we shut our minds to it and went on playing rugby as usual.' There are, however, important differences. No adolescent today believes in a wholly just war, let alone a war to end war; no one believes in the value of sacrifice as such; and no one believes that war would be followed by survival and peace.

This pessimism about the outcome of another global war was more prevalent in the early sixties than in the last year judging by school discussions. A positive attitude to death which has been expressed by young people concerns the disposal of the body and is in line with the adolescent desire to be of service to the community.

'My father has bequeathed his body to the anatomist,' announced a fifth-former in a grammar school. 'I think it's a most cheerful thing to do. I'd love to think of my old corpse still being of some use. You have to get a form and the next-of-kin sign it.'

'You can give your eyes to eye banks if you're quick about it,' another said. 'You can help to make the blind see.'

Another hope of the adolescent, as far as I can find out, lies in Space, particularly in the possibility of there being sentient beings elsewhere who have evolved farther than we have. No longer alone, our guides may come to us before we reach them. They may rescue us and, above all, give us the benefit of their advice. There is a future provided we don't blow ourselves up first, and even if we do the 'awareness' in the universe may not die out with man.

Fourteen

ATTITUDES TO WAR

Economists, psychologists, sociologists, the 'man in the street', pacifists, and generals, all have their own attitudes to war, including diagnosis of its causes, which most thinking adults now agree are complex and multiple. Neither an economic situation alone nor the aggressive impulses rooted in man's nature can wholly account for outbreaks of mass slaughter within the human species. People over fifty in England today can look back on a marked change in attitudes to war since the early years of the century, and this change is due to two things, in the main. Firstly, there has been the extension of warfare from a limited to a global scale, accompanied by the involvement of civilians, including women and children, as well as soldiers. This extension has also meant an increase in the use of scientific weapons of various kinds. Secondly, the depth and extent of the violence involved has horrified and astounded people who believed that human beings were 'progressing'. It has led some to take note of the new science of psychology and to ask if the 'dark side of man's nature' is bound to erupt at times; if, in fact, the human condition is, in essence, deplorable. In referring to war, Freud says that we are descended from a race of murderers, and, he might have added, from a particularly cruel type of murderer. No animal other than man has inflicted such detailed and diabolical suffering, even on children. It has even been justified in the name of ideologies.

In spite of the falling death rate from natural causes and the increasing expectation of life in all countries today which have made use of new medical knowledge and managed to create a higher standard of living, there is not less preoccupation with death but, rather, more. And one of the reasons for this is fear of, and remembrance of, war.

Before 1914 grandfathers told their grandchildren about the 'soldiers of the queen' dressed in scarlet and black tunics. Colourful pictures of the 'Battle of the Modder River' hung in parlours of the working class, and though nasty things happened in the Crimean War Florence Nightingale's lamp still shone and little girls were asked to emulate her. The Napoleonic Wars were history but Napoleon was a respected enemy—'Boney'—in a way which 'Kaiser Bill' rarely was, and Hitler never. Boys played with toy cannons and the little lead soldiers were infantry or cavalry. There were no airmen or tank corps. Some years earlier Mr Brontë had bought his son Branwell six glamorous toy soldiers in a wooden box and the Brontë children had played out their aggressions in the fantasies of Angola and the Gondals.

On May 24, 1914, in the council schools of England, little girls still wore white frocks and, round their necks, daisy chains, symbol of the Empire, and together with the boys with red, white, and blue streamers saluted the flag and sang Kipling's *Recessional* and *Land of Hope and Glory*.

Then in August came the First World War, which changed for ever attitudes to conflict in this and many other countries. The 1914 war started off with shock, indignation, and a mad burst of patriotism which was mingled with a good dose of hypocrisy, particularly in connection with the 'rape of dear little Belgium', which became personified almost in the form of that everlasting sister whom pacifists were believed to prefer to be raped rather than that they should be called upon to defend her honour. Boasts that the war would be over by Christmas, with the Kaiser 'licked'—this being a term used by ex-public schoolboys who had themselves submitted to the English form of school punishment—were accompanied by white feathers presented 'to conchies', mostly by the wives and mothers who were prepared to 'give' their sons and husbands. The terminology is important—e.g. the Kaiser 'licked' really meant slaughter of Germans, 'giving' sons really meant accepting the fact that your just grown-up boy was to be bayoneted through the abdomen or shot through the brain.

A child of 1914 found himself or herself expected to regard

the departure of father and brothers, the growing lists of casualties on our side, as 'sacrifices for the right'. There were no 'dead'; they were the 'Fallen'. The Tommies sent embroidered silk cards with flags of the glorious Allies home from the 'Front' and, home on leave, did not tell children what 'Front' meant in terms of Flanders mud and mangled bodies of dying boys, many not yet out of their teens. Schools acted playlets such as 'The Empire's Honour', in which Rhodesia was always the youngest child in a dear little white dress and England the Head Prefect holding a trident. In the tougher districts children made the streets noisy with songs, and even in the playgrounds teachers turned deaf ears to words which in peace-time might have been considered to merit corporal punishment:

> At the Cross, at the Cross,
> Where the Kaiser lost his hoss
> And the Eagle on his helmet flew away,
> He was eating German buns
> When he heard the British guns
> And the silly little bugger ran away.

Cowardice and atrocity were attributed to the enemy except among the very few enlightened ones. It was the Germans who spiked Belgian babies on their bayonets (why not believe this?—the children had also heard of the Massacre of the Innocents in Scripture lessons). Sometimes the noble Allies came under suspicion. Obviously the 'Wops' were not as brave as the British.

Rupert Brooke, to a more sophisticated and older group, expressed the mood of the earlier part of the War and the prevailing temper of some non-combatants throughout— 'Honour is come back, as a king to reign'—and when he died of a bite 'in some corner of a foreign field that is for ever England' he became the soldier-god.

To most of the children death had acquired various tags. It was 'death with honour', 'death for King and Country'. Sunday school teachers and preachers told them that the War could be likened to the Crucifixion—the 'boys in the trenches' were dying, as Christ did, to save mankind. They were your adolescent brothers one day, wanting a few fags and balaclavas; the next they were the 'immortal dead'.

But as the slaughter grew worse not even the Angels of Mons, or Jesus himself walking through the front lines, could hide the reality of death by killing. The mood of Brooke gave way to that of Owen, Sassoon, and others of the real war poets. Brooke's boys who 'gave their immortality' had changed into horrified men who had watched 'limbs knife-skewed' and those who had 'died in hell (they called it Passchendale)'.

When the disillusioned returned to find no homes for heroes, victory so wildly celebrated on November 11, 1918, passing into the Depression of the twenties, as the unemployed marched hungry to London and *Love on the Dole* was the play of the year, war for ever lost its glamour for the grown-ups and for a time at any rate some children were not encouraged to play with toy soldiers. But the real shock had yet to come, for it dawned on the survivors of the 'war to end wars' that yet another was looming on the horizon, that forces were gathering which appeared to be wholly evil; and this was when even the 'man in the street' began to ask from whence arise these destructive urges in human beings, are they ineradicable, are we all guilty, friend and enemy alike? Freudian psychology had reached England and nothing would be the same any more. Even Hitler could be explained in terms of paranoia.

The children of the Second World War were 'in it' to an extent that their predecessors in 1914 never were. The city lights were dimmed before September 3, 1939, and thousands of them were evacuated when the first sirens went, a small proportion over the Atlantic. Separation, so closely associated with death, became a prolonged reality. Even the under-fives, evacuated with such mothers as were willing, suffered an uprooting and separation from other members of the family.

Side by side with the growing horror of warfare was the gradual realization that millions of Jews were being massacred. Former pacifists threw in their lot with the armed forces and in this war, like the rehearsal for it, the Spanish

Civil War, there were probably more people consciously fighting for and against ideologies than in any previous ones. The interesting thing is that at the same time there was less hate, less mere patriotism, far more tolerance than in the First World War.

This affected the children. They played their war games with Germany as the enemy, they dug for victory, knitted scarves, collected waste-paper, but there was much more sympathy and understanding of other children, even of enemy ones. This new generation knew more about the world. Even if geography books full of patronizing and whimsical stories of 'little people of other lands' were still used in schools, radio gave them a more realistic impression of foreign children, whom they were learning to regard— in advance of the schools—not as quaint pets, nor as wild savages, but as children like themselves who wanted to live, play, grow up. All the same, there was still the belief that killing in warfare is justifiable and, as a speaker on the BBC Home Service put it, 'Children grew up with the terrible assumption that war was all right.' He described his own growing up during 1939–45: 'Three afternoons a week we went to the cinema and saw news-films of war and war was still glamorized . . . in church we prayed for victory.' There were two myths. (1) War is a sort of game. One can have fun. (2) Physical courage is the greatest kind. Growth to maturity, according to another speaker, was delayed by war. 'Will it ever be possible to stop juvenile violence when adult violence is put over as something laudable?'

Another interesting observation made during the war years was that it was not the Germans who were Enemy No 1 but the Japanese. At the time when some of the German atrocities against the Jews were at their peak both adults and children were heard to refer to the Japanese as 'slit-eyed yellow devils' and stories of jungle and prisoner-of-war atrocities abounded. It was the Japs, not the Germans, who were regarded almost as sub-human. Later, when the European war ended and the atom bombs were dropped on Hiroshima and Nagasaki, many people in this country suffered another 'change of heart'. At the time I happened to be with a group of adolescent boys and girls, who registered simple shock. They were silent for a long time as though experiencing an immediate bereavement.

Sylvia Anthony's book on *The Child's Discovery of Death* was published in June 1940, and the study on which it was based was finished early in 1939, so that only the earlier part of the Second World War had been experienced. In her Preface, Mrs Anthony says:

Although, looking back, men may see this period as part of an interval between two great wars, the lives and thoughts of English children were not, I believe, affected by war during the months when this study was made any more than is normal for children in democratic countries during the intervals of peace. Their behaviour, indeed, may in respect of the idea of death provide a standard against which those caring for children in war-time may roughly measure their reactions under unaccustomed stresses.

I believe that they will find that in war-time it is not so much aspects of death previously unrealized which distress the child as the changing of life-patterns in which his emotions have been anchored. Thus a little girl, accused of stealing from her billet-mother, told me: 'When my father told our John he was going in the army, he (John) started to cry.' 'Why?' 'Cos he wanted him to stop with my mother.' It is from complex miseries such as this that most childish neuroses in war-time arise. War and its demands fill our minds today. But experiences of alarm, danger, and utmost horror or grief appear to precipitate rather than initiate mental instability or disorder. Reactions in childhood to the idea of death, on the other hand, may lie at the very root of such morbid development. In the connection between the two an immense field lies open for exploration, almost untrodden. This study lies only at the gateway: yet it seemed to me that from this position one had a view of new scientific riches and new hopes for human happiness that lay beyond.

This was written over twenty-five years ago, since when we have been travelling through the period of the 'Cold War' interspersed with real local wars and bloody revolutions. There is an abundant literature of the Second World War covering fiction, biography, autobiography, letters, and memoirs, as well as in scientific surveys and sociological investigations published in both popular and technical journals and books. Children in evacuation were compared with children who stayed at home and suffered air raids. They were studied in schools, foster homes, hospitals, in age groups, sexes, at work and at play. In a recent edition of *The Natural Development of the Child* Agatha Bowley sums up some of these in her chapter on 'Children and War', adding her own findings. Referring to one of the better-known surveys, *The Cambridge Evacuation Survey*, she summarizes the most important findings as follows. The age group sevens to elevens settled down best, which appears to be in line with those who regard the junior school period as most stable. However, one is never quite sure what 'settling down' implies in this age which has not even yet received the detailed attention given to nursery infants and adolescents.

The second finding was that many adolescents were restless, wanting parents, home life and the city, the restlessness being regarded as more than the usual turbulence of their age group. Under-fives evacuated in nurseries showed signs of disturbance, but this, as one would expect, was not shown by children accompanied by their mothers. From this and other surveys conclusions were drawn that some children suffered more from separation from home and family than from fear of imminent death in air raids. But here again, unless the surveys are very comprehensive and deep, it is difficult to say what sort of fear children may feel in a given situation, and answers to direct questions may be evaded. A child, indeed, may appear to be less worried about its own death and even death of the family when they are 'all in together' in an air-raid shelter and more worried and disturbed by separation. But what does separation mean? To a young child it is like death, to the older one and the adolescent it may also include death, for the evacuated child may have worried a great deal about danger to those he had left behind in the bombed cities.

Reports from other countries where war was experienced by children directly during invasion and occupation, and from Jewish children, throw much more light on children's attitudes to death in warfare. It has been suggested that when Ann Frank, finally put into a concentration camp, witnessed the death of her sister her 'will to live' cracked, while we know from her diary that when she was in hiding with

L

her family fear of what might happen ultimately was in abeyance. Children whose parents were killed in front of them whether by so called legitimate enemy action or by assassination obviously suffered severe trauma, but fear of imminent death for oneself or relatives, as far as has been observed, causes only temporary disturbance in those who are stable otherwise.

Agatha Bowley quotes the investigations of Dr Burbary in the Manchester Child Guidance Clinic, who found that only 5 per cent of unevacuated children investigated exhibited new symptoms of disturbance after air raids compared with 17 per cent disturbances in the evacuated who had not been subjected to bombardment. Of 8,000 Bristol children only 3¾ per cent showed strain due to raids and in a small hospital group Bodman found that twenty-five out of forty-five showed distress for three weeks after severe bombing, only 5 for longer periods. Although one must accept to some extent that it has been shown that a stable child can recover from experiences such as being faced with death, it is extremely difficult to come to long-term conclusions unless such a child has been followed up to maturity. Nor, as has been mentioned before, can we draw too many conclusions from English children. All grown-ups who were in England during the last war remember what Sylvia Anthony calls the 'wild aggressions' of the Basque refugees. Those who worked during the post-war period in countries which had been occupied or where battles had actually been fought have described the 'docile' children still suffering from shock (certainly often combined with malnutrition) or, alternatively, the bands of homeless hooligans who wandered over Europe.

When we make generalizations about the effect of war on children we should realize that in terms of suffering we know little about it. What must the agony of the children in besieged cities have been like?

During the black famine of the winter there was nothing with which to heat the houses. Ink froze in pots at school. Teachers died. Children who kept coming to school survived, while many who stayed at home succumbed. Men and women who, even though they could hardly walk, persisted in reaching their place of work, going to meetings, had a better chance of survival than those who crept into a corner by themselves. Collectively, people's spirits held up longer. When they turned their back to the wall they died. . . .

Here is an extract from the diary of a schoolgirl, who perished from the effects of the siege.

> Jenia died on December 28th, 1941, at 12.30 a.m.
> Grandmother died on January 25th, 1942.
> Lena died on March 17th, 1942.
> Uncle Lesha died on May 10th at 4.00 p.m.
> May 13th, at 7.30 a.m., darling Mama died.
> The Saviches are dead, they all died.
> (*The Road to Volgograd*, by Alan Sillitoe, 1964)

In this country some of the evacuees wet their foster parents' beds, stole, and 'corrupted' the local children. Many went back, preferring air raids to life in the country. Those who constantly heard the sirens admitted to some fear (52 per cent in Agatha Bowley's survey) and most observers agree that most anxiety was shown, as Russell points out in *Children's Thinking*, after the age of thirteen.

In the children I have investigated for this study the most important finding to my mind is not that children today are bringing in physiological concepts earlier, nor that more preoccupation about death is shown both overtly and covertly by certain religious groups, but that there appears to be a correlation between high intelligence, creativity, and sensitivity and fear of death. The rosy, bounding seven-year-old illegitimate child who wished to remain at the age of twenty-one so that he 'would never have to die' followed it up by saying 'life is too nice—I never want to die'. Most of the children who overtly expressed fear of death explained this in terms of love of life.

For numbers of children throughout the world today 'the wild joys of living' exist and death is not a merciful release. Who wants to be slaughtered in the full flush of life? Secondly, people are no longer able to accept the idea that those who die in glory will put on immortality. Investigations of post-war students in the USA and in this country reveal very interesting changes in religious attitudes, but evidence and conclusions are conflicting. Allport, Gillespie,

and Young in 1948 found that 'war experiences were sufficiently traumatic to eradicate many juvenile conceptions of
religion (especially of prayer), but seven out of ten felt that
they needed 'some form of religious orientation in order to
achieve a fully mature philosophy of life' and 11 per cent
needed a 'new type of religion'. The spontaneous prayers for
help on the battlefield or during bombardment, together
with an increase in superstition, such as the wearing of
lucky charms, went on side by side with a fatalism revealed
by such remarks as 'If your number's on the bomb, then
you've had it.' These behaviour patterns simply reveal, in
one way and another, fear of death. The more alive and
happy the individual, the more he or she disliked the prospect of dying.

It is very difficult to discover how far war has entered into
the fantasies of the modern child and what it means. So
much that may appear to be significant to someone who goes
into a given school as a 'tester' may be found, later on, to be
directly related to what had just been read in a horror comic
or seen on television. Very few investigators can watch all
the programmes and read all the comics, glossy magazines,
and the gutter Press. Thus, a frieze of terrifying figures done
by a normal eight-year-old class was thought to have come
from a maladjusted school by an education department, and
a child who appeared to show a preoccupation with death
by strangling was regarded as psychotic. In each case there
was an immediate environmental reason for these manifestations, as in the 'Draw a Man' test which I carried out
in some Oxford junior schools and received drawings of
skeletons hung with CND badges.

There are actual wars and revolutions now and in the
living memories of today's young people—Hungary, Suez,
Angola, the Congo, Algeria, French Indo-China, Cyprus,
and Vietnam, and all the aggression connected with racial
problems. These are discussed by children from top juniors
onwards, and a number of them are not only seriously concerned but quite well informed. There is no doubt whatever
that owing to the new media of communication a much more
knowledgeable generation is growing up.

Another aspect of war which is being investigated is the possible effect of being a 'war baby' and spending the very early 'formative' years under conditions of stress. The babies of the Second World War are now between twenty-one and twenty-seven and some psychiatrists have claimed that these young people show signs of disturbance. Some relate it to the absence of the father. Much more would have to be discovered about the subsequent years of rapid change before one could relate later adolescent disturbance directly to father absence. Disturbance may occur in the father's presence too.

Economic deprivation, the absence of treats and luxuries, the general drabness of life can affect young children as adversely as some of the emotional deprivations. In any case, love cannot exist for very long if people's nerves are 'shot to pieces' by perpetual bombing, overwork, poor housing, and bad food. The mass killing which goes on in war also lowers the vitality of the populace after a time—life is reduced. It is most unlikely that in the event of a future world war one would be able to take the advice given by Agatha Bowley in her book produced during the last war. 'As adults', she wrote, 'we must try to teach them to regard the war as a glorious adventure, as a challenge and a spur to endeavour.' This would hardly have been the advice taken by post-Hiroshima children. Bowley also found that war-time drawings of the English children she investigated did not show any preoccupation with war. This is in marked contrast with children's pictures collected from war zones.

She says: 'Looking through these 183 drawings, or 82 per cent which bore no trace of the war, one felt these were still the piping days of peace. It was refreshing to find the children's outlook undaunted by the blackout or by clouds of war.' But children under the shadows of invasion, occupation, resistance movements, and concentration camps expressed themselves rather differently.

In January 1943, under the direction of the Refugee Children's Evacuation Fund, an exhibition of Children's Art was held in New Bond Street. Later a booklet was printed showing twenty of these pictures. One of the more arresting of these is called 'In Poland Now', by a Polish child aged thirteen, which is symbolic of death. The usual paraphernalia are there—the skeleton, scythe, etc—but what is so terrifying is the portrayal of two stars and a huge moon weeping tears over some houses. Another, entitled 'New Order', by an Austrian of seventeen years, shows the ghastly reality of the firing squad.

The horrors of the A-bomb on Hiroshima have also been recorded by schoolchildren who remembered what happened on August 6, 1945, when they were six years younger. Dr Osada collected 2,000 accounts of that day and from a selection published a book which first appeared in English translation in 1963 (*Children of the A-Bomb*; Peter Owen). There is practically no hatred shown in these writings—only plain horror of war:

'. . . Since my house was at Togiya, close to the place where the bomb fell, my mother was turned to white bones before the family altar. . . . When I think that for all those years I haven't been able to talk to mother I can hardly bear it' (eleven-year-old girl who was five in 1945).

'When we came to the river there was a man who was really suffering; he was black all over and he kept saying, "Give me water, give me water!" I felt so sorry for him I could hardly bear it. People were in the river drinking the river water. An air-raid warden was saying, "You mustn't drink the water." He was saying it, but people didn't pay any attention to him and lots of people kept going into the water and dying.

'Many little children were crying, "I'm hungry!" That's because they hadn't had their breakfast before the bomb fell. . . . At the end of August a baby was born. But only the baby's head was born, and then the baby and mother died together. I was terribly sad' (ten-year-old girl who was four in 1945).

'I really hate to think about war and I hate to remember the day when the atom bomb fell. Even when I read books I skip the part about war. And I shiver at the newsreels in the movies when the scenes of the war in Korea appear. Since I was assigned this for homework, and even though I don't want to do it, I am making myself remember that awful time' (eleven-year-old girl who was five in 1945).

'My little three-year-old brother, with his arms and legs all wrapped in bandages, used to run outside every time an aeroplane passed and shout: "Give back my sister! Give back my sister!" . . . This little brother, directing his babyish anger at the aeroplanes that had carried away the big sister who loved him, afraid even to look up at the sky—probably after that he did not enjoy a single happy moment, and there was no way to have a first-rate doctor to look after him—on the 22nd of October, as mother held him tightly in her arms, he departed to follow our sister' (seventeen-year-old boy who was eleven at the time of the bomb).

'Can you imagine what a hard time Father and I have getting along? And how many people were made even more unfortunate than us? I who know the evil of the atom bomb believe that we must make another bloody war impossible. I pray that everyone will remember that 6th of August so that there will be lasting peace' (fifteen-year-old boy who was nine at the time of the bomb).

'At the side of the Kyobashi River, burned people were moaning "Hot! Hot!" and jumping into the river, and since they could not move their bodies freely they would call for help with the voices of those facing death and drown. The river became not a stream of flowing water but rather a stream of drifting dead bodies. No matter how much I might exaggerate the stories of the burned people who died shrieking and of how the city of Hiroshima was burned to the ground, the facts would still be more clearly terrible and I could never really express the truth on this piece of paper; on this point I ask for pardon. Looking at this pitiable scene, I wondered why human beings who ought to be of the same mind have to make wars; why they have to kill each other like this' (sixteen-year-old boy who was ten at the time of the bomb).

Fifteen

CONCLUSION

All those who come into close contact with children will need no convincing by detailed statistical evidence that from a very early age in this country they are interested in death. It would appear from the work of Nagy and others, including some studies of primitive societies, that though the framework may differ the picture of the growing child seems to be basically the same throughout the world. The healthy child is both curious and fearful, he passes through immature stages before he develops an understanding of death, and adult concepts may not only be meaningless but confusing. My own observations have led me to believe that over the present century there has not been very much change in children's basic attitudes in spite of the differences between the social, scientific, and religious backgrounds of today as compared with the early war period (1940), when Sylvia Anthony wrote *The Child's Discovery of Death*, or even much farther back, when Sully produced *Studies of Childhood*. Up to the end of the junior school children still tend to accept the attitudes of adults, and as long as we have religious instruction many of them will produce stereotyped pictures of heaven and angels, and God with a beard; infants will write prayers to a father God and Jesus. But there is a great deal of evidence that by adolescence the children are sceptical, often in a dangerous and destructive sense, which brings with it an exaggerated distrust of grown-ups and may underlie some of the more aggressive acts of today's teenagers. It seems to me that there is no evidence that religious attitudes have ever made a child feel more secure or have consoled him. They have often frightened him. We no longer find children who are terrified by hell-fire because the most rigidly theological of the adults is unlikely to believe in the doctrine which was not uncommon at the end of the last century. We belong to the post-Freud age and no one would dare to write anything like the following passage:

In the fifth dungeon, a red hot oven, is a little child. Hear how it screams to come out, see how it turns and twists itself about in the fire: it beats its head against the roof of the oven. It stamps its little feet on the floor of the oven. To this child God was very good. Very likely God saw that this child would get worse and worse and would never repent, and so it would have to be punished much more in hell. So God in his mercy called it out of the world in its early childhood.

Quoted from 'The Sight of Hell' by J. Furnise, SJ, in a book *Is Death the End of All Things for Man*, by 'A parent and teacher' (1870).

But although God as aggressor is certainly much less evident now, children may still think of death as an act of aggression, and if they have been taught to believe in a very much personified deity they will naturally endow him with the kind of aggression which they understand.

'Help! Help!' cried out a little girl, nearly four, who was playing with a doll in the Wendy house in a nursery school (January 21, 1965). 'Jesus is calling my baby to Heaven. Quick, quick or it will die.' This not only shows confusion but a healthy desire to thwart the aggression of Jesus. Recent work in the USA has confirmed that children regard God, who 'takes' people away to heaven, as a murderer.

Perhaps the change which has most influenced children's attitudes to death and will do so even more in the next half-century is the emphasis on science, which is already being introduced into the curriculum of the primary school. Although these younger children are not sufficiently mature to be influenced by some of the contemporary religious concepts, and could scarcely find any meaning in such ideas as that of union with the 'divine ground' or immortality as 'the eternal now', they already do find meaning in some scientific concepts by the age of about nine. Thus the fact of bodily change at death, whether by slow disintegration in the ground or by quick combustion into ashes and gases, excites their interest and appears to be reassuring when they are able to link this with the idea of 'becoming one with Nature'.

Children are less likely now to be reassured by the supernatural, if ever they were, and one finds it difficult to believe that any child would really be excited by the idea of a 'resurrection body'. In this country the sociological background does not appear to influence children's ideas of death directly, mainly because even in the poorer areas life can be good at times, at least until later adolescence, and with the exception of some coloured children there is no evidence of any desire for the after-life as portrayed in religions. There are more' overt expressions of violence in some of these areas, though according to an article in the *Twentieth Century* (Winter, 1964–5) by Peter Way, who has worked in Eton, dockland, and new town schools, children in all areas adopt an 'eye for an eye' philosophy when asked about such things as capital punishment. He suggests a difference in attitude in progressive schools which is in accord with my own observations. Linked perhaps indirectly with the social background, however, is the intellectual capacities of the child, which recent surveys have shown are more environmentally determined than was once thought to be the case, and as far as my investigations go it is the more 'gifted' children who are the strongest dislikers and fearers of death. This is in line with some American work on exceptional children. To quote just one of these, published in 1961, Freehill in *Gifted Children* describes a very intelligent boy of four years who became extremely agitated on overhearing a conversation between two adolescent boys. 'Did you hear what that boy said?' he asked his mother, but it was not until next morning that he finally whispered to her the dread words. 'The boy said "See you tomorrow, if I'm still alive".' Then, agitatedly, 'Mother, is he? Is he, Mother?' His dread of death was found to have been triggered off by an earlier experience when he and an older child had found a bone which the eight-year-old had said would make you die if you touched it.

Freehill gives evidence in this book to support the contention that more intelligent children have such fears earlier than the less intelligent. Some of these early fears concern 'surgery, death, war, and traffic'. Their lives being so rich, death is seen as an even greater deprivation. Many parents have noticed that at first, when their children are very young, they try to discover in death an element of fair play. It is the old who usually die first, and that is as it should be. Several parents have described heated quarrels among siblings as to whom will die first, the slightly older one being furious at being told by a younger one that he will die 'long before me'. The death of young people is either regarded as unfair or more often as the person's own fault, especially if it is an accident. The attitudes of the less able children are more liable to lead them to accept death as 'all being in the same boat together' and 'when your number's up it's up—you've had it'. This attitude is perhaps the most common among grown-ups. In *The Shape of Death*, by Jaroslav Pelikan, in 1962, which is written from a religious angle, the author also puts this point of view—'whenever death comes one consolation is always the vast and brilliant company of those who have suffered the same fate'. The feeling that at death one is 'with the ages' is rarely expressed except in imitation by children, though it can be an inspiring thought to some adults, especially when it is someone else who has died. By and large, then, the main conclusion of this book is that death is regarded by children and many adults as a deprivation, and as long as it is the final, unchallenged end of man it is the major deprivation. Although in some cases, where people are grossly under-privileged or handicapped, ill or very old, death may appear preferable to life—and even children appreciate this—in general the human species, with its awareness and foreknowledge of death, is suffering from a deep sense of insecurity which starts as soon as the child discovers that the duration of life for himself and others is uncertain.

Even in children of quite an early age the death of 'the loved one' may be dreaded far more than death of the self, and later on, with the coming of marriage and parenthood, this is nearly always so. Thanatos is the major enemy not only of Eros but of love in all its multifarious shapes. Perfect faith may cast out fear, but perfect love cannot, for it is in the nature of love to require the presence of the beloved. Those capable of the deepest love, whether it be the love between the sexes, between parent and child, child and parent, friend and friend, will suffer most from bereavement, and though they may adjust in various ways to this major deprivation, to accept it as if it were good instead of evil is no more a sign of maturity than is the acceptance of poverty.

In bringing up our children at home and in the school there is one sure way of reducing the sadness of separation, and even the fear of one's own death. We can diminish love. We can so emphasize the group, the community, the State, that the individual loses his identity. We can get rid of the family or extend it until it becomes meaningless. We can discourage great friendships between children, can ridicule lovers, psychoanalyse the bereaved, underplay the emotions, dilute them in the community—there are thousands of ways of diminishing love. We can

> Sterilize mother's milk, spoon out
> The waters of comfort in Kilograms,
> Let Creation's pulse keep Greenwich Time,
> Let Love be clinic . . .

Or we can concentrate on getting rid of death as an inevitable event even though it may take millions of years. We can explore it, crack its code, try to conquer it as we are trying to conquer Space. If we choose this second alternative, we shall at the same time affirm a belief in the value of love. As teachers our philosophy of education will be positive and forward-looking and to some degree we shall be able to allay the fears and anxieties concerning death which children share with us at the present day. By recognizing that such fears are right and proper, natural to man, in no way anything to be ashamed of, to be discussed openly, we shall help children to get rid of guilt feelings associated with them and also to face up to the fact that preoccupation with violence, particularly of killing, springs from repressed fear. By examining death scientifically and showing children that it is a problem to be solved like that of 'how heredity works' we shall use their natural curiosity and overcome some of their repugnance by arousing and fostering their urges to explore the unknown. This is not as fantastic as it may sound and should not be dismissed as being in the realm of science-fiction. It has been seriously discussed by reputable scientists and references have been made to it in the Press and on television and radio. In the first chapter it was mentioned as an idea which is spreading in parts of America. The conquest of death as we know it, however, would occur in the far distant future, to other men and in an age which we can only imagine. Meanwhile we and our children have to die.

Another way of overcoming children's natural fears of death is to encourage them to create in art, poetry, music, and dance. In that way we shall help them to counteract the negative and destructive. Even if we cannot yet get rid of the last enemy we can at least affirm life and help children to live more abundantly.

But this is not enough. Until the time comes when scientists may discover how to make death a reversible instead of an irreversible reaction we must help children to realize how important it is to reduce the number of unnecessary deaths—deaths caused by disease, by low living standards, by avoidable accidents, by violence, and by warfare. We have health programmes in schools which point out the dangers of smoking, of not taking advantage of immunization, but so far a school which pointed out the dangers of fall-out would probably be held to be guilty of indoctrination.

Finally, if we can cast out all dogmas from our schools, clear the debris of the past, we may help children to realize that we are standing on a threshold even more exciting than when man first explored the unknown seas. We may tell them that our individual lives are part of something which will probably 'make sense' when we have solved the problems of the origin of life, the mechanics of the cell, and discovered the universe 'teeming with life'. However it all started, if it had a beginning, however it may end, if it will have an ending, the cosmos is strange, magnificent, exciting, true, and human history has a significant place in it. Otherwise, why have we become interpreters?

We do not have to accept the universe blindly, un-critically, helplessly, and we are doing no service to education if we bring up children to believe that human fears and anxieties about death are unfounded, that an undemonstrable belief is factually true, or that any human being up to date has revealed the total truth.

BIBLIOGRAPHY

of books and journals referred to in the text (arranged under authors)

ALEXANDER, I. E., and ADLERSTEIN, A. M. 'Studies in the Psychology of Death', *Journal of Genetic Psychology* (1960); also *Journal of Psychology* (1957), with COLLEY.

ALLPORT, GILLESPIE, and YOUNG. *Journal of Psychology* (1948), No. 48.

ANTHONY, S. *The Child's Discovery of Death.* (Kegan Paul, 1940.)

ARTHUR, B., and KEMME, M. *Journal of Child Psychology and Psychiatry.* (June, 1964), Vol. 5, No. 1.

BARRATT, E. *The Cry of the Children.* Complete Poems. (Chapman & Hall, 1856.)

BENEDICT, R. *Patterns of Culture.* (Routledge, 1935.)

BODMAN, F. 'War Conditions and the Mental Health of the Child', *British Medical Journal,* October 4, 1941, pp. 486–8.

BOWLBY, J., and FRY, M. *Child Care and the Growth of Love.* (Pelican, 1953.)

BOWLBY, J. *The International Journal of Psychoanalysis.* (1961.)

BOWLEY, A. *The Natural Development of the Child.* (E. & S. Livingstone, 1948.)

CARDUS, N. *Autobiography.* (Collins, 1947.)

COUSINET, R. *La Vie sociale des enfants.* (Paris, 1950.)

DARLINGTON, C. H. *The Facts of Life.* (Allen & Unwin, 1953.)

DAVIES, W. H. *Autobiography of a Super-Tramp.* (Cape, 1955.)

DE LA MARE, W. *Early One Morning.* (Faber & Faber, 1935.)

DOUGLAS, J. W. B. *The Home and School* (MacGibbon & Key, 1964.)

DURKHEIM, E. *Le Suicide.* (Paris, 1897. English trans by J. A. Spaulding and George Simpson; Routledge & Kegan Paul, 1952.)

ERIKSON, E. H. 'Psychology', *Journal of Social Issues,* Vol. 1 (i).

ETTINGER, R. *The Prospect of Immortality.* (Sidgwick & Jackson, 1965.)

FREEHILL. *Gifted Children.* (Collier–Macmillan, 1961.)

FREUD, S. *Civilization, War and Death.* Ed. by John Richman. Psychoanalytical Epitomes, No. 4. (Hogarth Press, 1952.)

FREUD, S. *Totem and Taboo.* Trans. by J. Strachey. (Routledge & Kegan Paul, 1960.)

GESELL, A. *The First Five Years.* (New York: Harper, 1940.)

GESELL, A., ILLIG, BATES-AMES, etc. *Youth.* (Harper & Bros, 1956.)

GORER, G. *Death, Grief and Mourning in Contemporary Britain.* (Cresset Press, 1965.)

GORER, G. *Exploring English Character.* (Cresset Press, 1955.)

GRIFFITHS, R. *Imagination and Play in Early Childhood.* (Kegan Paul, 1938.)

HALL, S. *Adolescence: Its Psychology and its Relations to Physiology, Anthropology, Sociology, Sex, Crime, and Education.* (1904.)

HALL, S. *American Journal of Psychology.* (1915.)

HARRISON, T. H. *Britain Revisited.* (Gollancz, 1961.)

HEMMING, J. *Problems of Adolescent Girls.* (Heinemann, 1960.)
HIMMELWEIT, OPPENHEIM, and VINCE. *Television and the Child.* (OUP, for the Nuffield Foundation, 1958.)
HOURD, M. L., and COOPER, G. E. *Coming into their Own.* (Heinemann, 1959.)
ILLIG and BATES-AMES. *Child Behaviour.* (Hamish Hamilton, 1955.)
ISAACS, S. *The Social Development of Children.* (Routledge, 1940.)
JACKSON, B., and MARSDEN, D. *Education and the Working Class.* (Routledge & Kegan Paul, 1952.)
JACKSON, L. (ELISAVETA FEN). *A Russian Childhood.* (Methuen, 1961.)
JAMES, E. O. *Beginnings of Religion.* (Hutchinson, 1958.)
JEPHCOTT, SEEAR, and SMITH. *Married Women Working.* (Allen & Unwin, 1962.)
KINGSLEY, C. *Letters and Memories.* (H. S. King, 1877.)
KNIGHT, M. *Humanist Anthology.* (Barrie & Rockliff, 1961.)
LASKI, M. *Ecstasy.* (Cresset Press, 1961.)
LAWRENCE, FRIEDA. *Memories and Correspondence.* (Heinemann, 1961.)
LEAVIS, F. R. *The Common Pursuit.* (Chatto & Windus, 1952.)
LEWIS, C. S. *Surprised by Joy.* (Collins, 1959.)
LOUKES, H. *Teenage Religion in 1961.* (SCM Press, 1963.)
MANNIN, E. *Confessions and Impressions.* (Hutchinson, 1963.)
MEAD, M. *Coming of Age in Samoa.* (1963.) *Growing up in New Guinea.* (1954.) Reprinted in Pelican for Penguin Books.
MITFORD, J. *The American Way of Death.* (Hutchinson, 1963.)
MUMFORD, L. *The Conduct of Life.* (Secker, 1952.)
MURRAY, JAMES. *The Juvenile Keepsake.* (1850.)
NAGY, M. *Journal of Genetic Psychology* (1948), vol 73.
NEWSOM (Report). *Half Our Future.* (HMSO, 1963.)
OPIE, I., and P. *The Lore and Language of Schoolchildren.* (Clarendon Press, 1959.)
OSADA, A. Compiler of *Children of the A-Bomb.* (Peter Owen, 1963.)
PELIKAN, J. *The Shape of Death.* (Macmillan, 1962.)
PIAGET, J. *The Child's Conception of the World.* (Kegan Paul, 1929.)
PIAGET, J. *Language and Thought of the Child.* 3rd Edn. (Routledge & Kegan Paul, 1959.)
POPPER, KARL. *The Open Society and its Enemies.* (Routledge & Kegan Paul, 1952.)
RICHARDSON, M., and TOYNBEE, P. *Thanatos.* (Gollancz, 1963.)
REICH, W. *The Sexual Revolution.* Trans. Theodore P. Wolfe. (Orgone Inst. Press, 1945.)
REID, A. *Philosophy and Education.* (Heinemann, 1962.)
ROBINSON, J. A. T. *Honest to God.* (SCM Press, 1963.)
RUSSELL, D. H. *Children's Thinking.* (Ginn.)
RUSSELL, BERTRAND. *What I Believe.* (Kegan Paul, 1925.)
RUTHERFORD, D., Trans. *Vor Tag (The Threshold).* (Kegan Paul, 1955.)
SILLITOE, A. *The Road to Volgograd.* (1964.)
STENGEL, E. *Suicide and Attempted Suicide.* (Pelican, 1964.)
SULLY, J. *Studies of Childhood.* (Longmans, Green & Co, 1895.)
THOMAS, DYLAN. *Collected Poems.* (Dent, 1953.)
WADDINGTON. *The Nature of Life.* (Allen & Unwin, 1961.)
WILLIAMS, E. *George.* (Hamish Hamilton, 1961.)
WOLFENSTEIN, M. *Disaster.* International Library of Sociology and Social Reconstruction. (Routledge & Kegan Paul, 1957.)
WYNN, M. *Fatherless Families.* (Michael Joseph, 1964.)